*The International*
# Dictionary
of
# Personal Finance

# The International Dictionary of Personal Finance

**A J Rider**

**Revised by David Brighouse**

Apart from any fair dealing for the purpose of research or private study, or criticism or review, as permitted under the Copyright, Designs and Patents Act 1988, this publication may only be reproduced, stored or transmitted, in any form or by any means, with the prior permission in writing of the publisher, or in the case of reprographic reproduction in accordance with the terms and licences issued by the Copyright Licensing Agency. Enquiries concerning reproduction outside those terms should be addressed to the publisher. The address is below.

Global Professional Publishing Limited
Random Acres
Slip Mill Lane
Hawkhurst
Cranbrook
Kent TN18 5AD

http: www.gppbooks.com

© Global Professional Publishing 2010
New Edition 2010

The moral right of the author has been asserted.
All rights reserved. No part of this book may be reproduced in any form or by any means without permission in writing from the publisher, except by a reviewer who may quote brief passages in a review.

ISBN: 978-1-906403-06-5

Typeset by Kevin O'Connor

Printed in India by Replika Press Pvt. Ltd.

---

For full details of Global Professional Publishing titles in Finance and Banking see our website at:
www.gppbooks.com

# Preface

The definitions given in this new edition of *The International Dictionary of Personal Finance* are as up-to-date as they can be in today's very fast moving world of personal finance. They cover the most common terms used in the United States and the United Kingdom. Where these are different they are marked in the entry with **[US]** or **[UK]** to indicate which country is relevant.

In deciding on which terms to include we have erred on the side of inclusiveness – obviously anything relating to pensions, mortgages, social benefits, personal taxation and inheritance is included but so are some of the slightly more esoteric terms which you might come across in dealings with a financial adviser.

If you spot a mistake, think the dictionary could be improved by changing a definition or wish to add something new, please let us know at the address on the opposite page or email me at sales@gppbooks.com and we'll see if we can incorporate your change in the next edition.

## abandonment [USA]
The voluntary relinquishing of all rights, title or possession of property such as trademarks, copyrights and patents etc.
**[UK]** A situation where an *option holder* allows ownership of an option to expire unexercised. Known in the USA as a *lapsed option*.

## acceptance
The writing of the word 'accepted' on the face of a *bill of exchange* by the drawee together with his/her signature indicating acceptance to pay the bill when due.

## accepting house [UK]
An organisation, usually a *merchant bank*, which accepts or guarantees *bills of exchange*.

## Access
A former *credit card* system which was sold to *Mastercard* and discontinued.

## accident insurance
*Insurance* which pays benefits in the event of an accident. Items typically covered are medical expenses and loss of earnings. If, for example, the insured sustains the loss of a limb or an eye, a specified lump sum is payable.

## accidental death insurance
*Insurance* which pays a lump sum in the event of death of the insured being caused by an accident.

## account
1. A facility, provided by financial institutions such as banks, in which an individual can keep money.
2. An itemised statement of money owed for the supply of goods or services.

## account balance [USA]
The net credit or debit balance of an *account* at the end of a reporting period.

## Accounting Standards Board [UK]
Since 1990, the UK body that sets standards for business accounting practices.

## account payee [UK]
Also 'account payee only.' Words written on the face of a cheque between two parallel vertical or diagonal lines. The purpose is to ensure that the cheque may only be paid into an account in the name of the payee, that is the person to whom the cheque is made payable. This means that the payee cannot sign it in favour of another person.

## accounts payable
Amounts owed by an organisation or individual to another for goods or services it has received.

## accounts receivable
Amounts due to an organisation or individual from another for goods or services it has supplied.

## accrual
A term used in company accounts where income is due or a cost is incurred during an accounting period but has not been received or paid.

## Act of God

**accrued benefits**
Benefits earned by an employee in respect of his/her pension based on years of service with his/her employer. The rate at which benefits accrue (e.g. 1/60th per year of membership) is called the accrual rate.

**accumulated dividend**
A dividend due to holders of *cumulative preferred stock* (USA) or *cumulative preference shares* (UK) but not yet paid. The amount is carried forward on the books as a liability until paid.

**accumulation [USA]**
Regular investment in a *mutual fund* with dividends reinvested.

**accumulation units [UK]**
Units in a *unit trust* where dividends, less basic rate tax, paid by companies in which the trust invests, are reinvested to increase the fund's unit value rather than distributed to unit-holders.

**acid test**
See *liquidity ratio*.

**acquisition**
A term used to describe the takeover of a company by another.

**Act of God**
An unpreventable and unpredictable event which could cause loss or damage to buildings, land, vehicles etc. Acts of God can be insurable.

## actuals
Commodities such as metals, coffee and grain which are bought and sold for use as opposed to *hedging* by trading on a *futures contract*.

## actuary
A person trained and specialising in risk, statistics and finance, qualified to give technical advice on insurance and pension business. Calculations made by actuaries include such items as premiums, bonus payments and life expectancy.

## A-Day [UK]
6th April 2006, the date when comprehensive pension reforms were introduced. The purpose was to simplify and streamline the system, standardising elements such as retirement age, the permitted amounts of individuals' tax-sheltered funds and contribution levels.

## additional personal allowance [UK]
Formerly an income tax allowance to certain single persons supporting a child at their own expense. Withdrawn from April 2000.

## additional state pension [UK]
See *S2P*.

## additional voluntary contributions (AVC)
Additional payments to a *tax deferred* savings account or an *occupational pension scheme* by an employee to boost a pension at retirement.

## adjustable rate mortgage (ARM) [USA]
A *mortgage* where the interest rate is liable to change over the term of the loan, dependent on influences such as interest rates on US *Treasury securities*.

## adjustable rate preferred stock (ARPS) [USA]
*Preferred stock* which pays a dividend in line with interest rates generally rather than a fixed dividend.

## adjusted gross income [USA]
A person's income on which federal income tax is calculated. This is *gross income* less adjustments such as Individual Retirement Account, Simplified Employee Pension Plan, *Keogh Plan* and *alimony* payments but before itemized deductions such as state and local income taxes, interest expenses and medical expenses.

## administrator (feminine form administratrix)
An individual legally appointed by a court to settle the affairs of a deceased person who failed to make a will, based on the rules of intestacy (see *intestate*). An administrator is also appointed in cases where the deceased person made a will but failed to name an *executor* or the executor predeceased or fails to act for some other reason.

## advisory account [UK]
An individual's account with a stockbroker where both advice is given and dealing conducted if required.

## affidavit
A written statement signed on oath and witnessed by an authorised person such as a notary public (USA) or a commissioner for oaths, invariably a solicitor (UK).

## affinity card
Credit card linked to a particular organisation, such as a business or a charity.

## after hours deals
Dealings made on a stock exchange after its official closure time. These deals are rolled over and included in the following day's transactions.

**age admitted [UK]**
A term used on occasions in *life assurance* policy documents, which indicates that the *life assured* has provided proof of his/her age by giving sight of his/her birth certificate to the insurance company. This means that no further evidence of age will be needed in the event of a claim.

**age allowance [UK]**
An additional personal allowance for persons aged 65 to 74 regarding income tax. A further increase in age allowance is applicable for persons aged 75 and over.

**agency**
A business operated by an *agent* in conjunction with his/her *principal*.

**agency securities [USA]**
Securities issued by federal government agencies.

**agent**
A person appointed by a *principal* to act on the latter's behalf in business.

**aggressive growth fund [USA]**
A *mutual fund* which invests in the stocks of rapid growth companies. Such companies pay little or no dividends, the prime purpose of this type of fund being to achieve greater than average capital appreciation. However the investment risk is correspondingly greater. Also known as maximum capital gains fund or capital appreciation fund.

**alimony**
Money paid to a divorced or separated spouse according to a divorce order. Known in the UK as maintenance payments.

## Alternative Investment Market

**allocation notice (assignment form/notice)**
A formal notification to the *writer* of an *option* from a clearing house (corporation) that an option has been exercised by an option *holder* and that the writer is obliged to buy/sell the *underlying instrument* at the *exercise price* to meet his/her obligations.

**allotment**
The distribution of shares to applicants. This may be for the full amount or, if *oversubscribed*, a proportion of the full amount.

**allotment notice/letter**
A confirming document from the company concerned that newly issued shares have been allotted to the applicant.

**allowances [UK]**
Amounts which may be deducted from a person's *gross income* prior to calculation of income tax. For example *personal allowance*. See *deduction* [UK].

**allowable expenses**
Expenses incurred by a person whilst carrying out duties at work, which are 'approved' by the tax authorities and can be offset against income to reduce taxable pay.

**alpha shares [UK]**
A term previously given to the most actively traded shares on the *London Stock Exchange* along with beta, gamma and delta shares. This classification was replaced by the *normal market size* classification in January 1991.

**Alternative Investment Market (AIM) [UK]**
A market for small, young and growing companies operated by the *London Stock Exchange* as a regulated market of a

*Recognised Investment Exchange* and set up in June1995. It effectively replaced the *Unlisted Securities Market (USM)*. The market provides an opportunity for companies to raise capital for expansion, a trading facility and a way of establishing a market value for their shares.

## alternative minimum tax (AMT) [USA]
A tax which targets high wealth individuals to pay a minimum amount of tax. The tax is calculated on the sum of adjusted gross income and tax preference items less exemptions.

## American Association of Individual Investors
A non-profit organisation located in Chicago whose purpose is to provide information and education regarding stocks, mutual funds and bonds etc to individual investors.

## American depositary receipt (ADR) [USA]
A receipt for the shares of a foreign company. The share certificate is issued and held by an American bank.

## American Express (AmEx)
An international company whose services include travel and financial products and which is probably most well known for the American Express *charge card* which enables the holder to obtain goods and services without the need to pay cash. Invoices of transactions are tendered monthly which must be settled in full. There is no preset spending limit.

## American Stock Exchange (AMEX)
A stock exchange located in Manhattan where stocks of small to medium sized companies are traded. In October 2008 it was acquired by NYSE Euronext and renamed NYSE Alternext US.

## annual percentage rate

### American style option
An *option* which may be exercised by the holder into its *underlying instrument* at any time until expiry. See also European style option.

### amortisation
The reducing of the value of an asset to zero over a period of time.

### analyst
A person who analyses data relevant to a subject such as securities in order to make recommendations.

### angel [USA]
1. An *investment grade* bond.
2. A provider of *venture capital*.

[UK] A provider of capital for theatrical productions.

### annual meeting [USA] annual general meeting (AGM) [UK]
An annual meeting, called by the directors of a company, which shareholders are invited to attend. Subjects normally discussed include audited accounts, election or re-election of directors and dividend payments to shareholders.

### annual percentage rate (APR)
Where interest on loans is expressed as other than a yearly rate, for example 1.5% per month, APR is the equivalent rate over a year, in this case 19.56%*. This enables would be borrowers to compare rates and to see the true extent of the rate of interest repayment they would incur.

\* To calculate APR
$$r = 100 [(1 + i/100) - 1]^m$$
where r = effective annual rate (APR) as a percentage

i = the period rate (for example 1.5 % in the example above)
m = number of periods in a year (for example 12 for a monthly rate)
In the UK, APR has a specific legal meaning, defined by the Consumer Credit Acts: its calculation incorporates certain other costs of borrowing in addition to the interest rate, in order to provide a comparison of the true cost of borrowing.

### annual report
A statement of a corporation's or company's performance over a year together with the accounts which is sent to shareholders.

### annual return [USA]
The total annual return on an investment which includes dividend payments and capital gains/losses. Not included are transactions costs and taxes.

**[UK]**
1. Another term for a person's yearly *tax return*.
2. An obligatory return, submitted annually to the *Registrar of Companies*, detailing information regarding a company's operations including business description, details of directors and company secretary, share capital etc.

### annuitant
A person in receipt of an *annuity*.

### annuitize [USA]
The commencement of regular payments from capital which has accumulated in an *annuity*.

### annuity [USA]
A type of contract in which an individual (the annuitant) builds up capital (tax deferred) in a savings account with a

## annuity

life insurance company, usually for retirement income. At retirement, the annuitant then begins drawing an income (known as annuitizing) which is subject to tax. There are two main types, fixed annuity and variable annuity. A **fixed annuity** guarantees payments which are fixed for life or a specific period. With a **variable annuity** payments to the annuitant vary and will depend on the performance of the insurance company's underlying investments.

[UK] The payment of a regular income from a life company to an annuitant in exchange for a lump sum either for life or shorter periods. Annuities are typically used for pensions and the individual receiving the annuity is known as an *annuitant*. In the UK they can broadly be classified into two types, compulsory purchase annuity and purchased life annuity. A **compulsory purchase annuity** is bought from the proceeds of a *pension* fund and is taxable as earned income. A **purchased life annuity** is bought with an individual's own capital and is subject to a more relaxed tax regime than a compulsory purchase annuity. There are three different types of annuities commonly referred to as standard annuities, with profits annuities and unit linked annuities. **Standard annuities** are the most commonly purchased and account for over ninety percent of the UK market. The income from a standard annuity is guaranteed for the rest of the annuitant's life whereas the income from a **with profits** or **unit linked annuity** will fluctuate depending on the investment performance of the underlying assets. There are various options which can be provided including, **annuity certain**: Income is paid for a given period whether or not death of the individual occurs. **deferred annuity**: Income which does not commence until some future specified date. **escalating annuity**: Income which increases annually by a given amount, for example 3%. The choosing of this option results in lower income compared with a level annuity over the initial years. **immediate annuity**: An annuity which starts to pay income soon after it has come into operation, for example at the end of the month following the payment of the lump sum. **joint life annuity**: Income usually relevant to two persons (for example man and wife) which continues until the death of the first person only. **joint life and survivor annuity**: Income usually relevant to two persons (for example man and wife) which continues until the death of the second person. **level annuity**: Income which is paid at a fixed rate throughout the life of the individual. See also *guaranteed minimum period*. **temporary annuity**: Income is paid either for a fixed period or until earlier death.

### annuity certain
See *annuity*.

### annuity starting date
The date on which annuity benefit payments commence to an annuitant.

### appropriate personal pension plan [UK]
A pension plan in which employer and employee pay full rate *National Insurance* contributions equivalent to the employee contracting into *S2P*. This rate will clearly be greater than the rate paid by contracting out of S2P. The difference between these rates, the contracted-out rebate, is paid by the Department for Work and Pensions (DWP) into a scheme known as an appropriate personal pension plan which buys pension benefits at retirement age known as *protected rights*. Provided an employee qualifies, incentive payments may also be paid by the DWP into the scheme. The contracted-out rebate plus any incentive payments are known as minimum contributions. Payment of minimum contributions into an appropriate personal pension plan results in a reduction of S2P benefit at retirement age as though the employee had contracted out through a *final salary* related scheme.

## approved investment trust [UK]
An *investment trust* which satisfies certain conditions set by the tax authorities and accordingly is exempt from tax on capital gains made on profits from sales of investments within its portfolio.

## approved list [USA]
A list of investments in which a financial institution such as a *mutual fund* is authorised to invest.

## arbitrage
The exploitation of price differentials between one market and another by simultaneously purchasing in one and selling in the other, such items as *commodities*, exchange rates, stocks etc.

## arbitrageur
A person or firm carrying out *arbitrage*.

## arrearage [USA]
The amount of interest due on bonds and dividends due on *cumulative preferred stock* but as yet unpaid. Whilst dividends on cumulative preferred stock remain unpaid, dividends on *common stock* are not payable.

## articles of association [UK]
The document which lists the regulations that govern the running of a company which include shareholder's voting rights, directors duties and general working and management etc. They are registered with the *memorandum of association* when the company is formed

## articles of incorporation [USA]
The document which the founders of a corporation submit to the relevant state for approval after which a certificate of incorporation is issued. These two documents form the

corporation's charter which endorses its legality. Information listed in the charter includes the name of the corporation, purpose, number of authorised shares and details of directors. The rules under which the corporation's internal management operates are listed in the *bylaws*.

**ask price**
The price at which a seller will trade a security or commodity. Also known as offer price.

**assay**
The testing of a metal to determine its degree of purity or to establish the constituents of an alloy (a mixture of metals).

**asset allocation**
The proportion of money allocated to various investments such as bonds, stocks, real estate and cash etc.

**assets**
Possessions owned by individuals or businesses having a monetary value. A corporation's assets can be referred to as tangible and intangible. Tangible assets include debtors, cash, stock and machinery etc. Intangible assets are those which cannot be seen and include such items as goodwill and patents.

**assignee**
A person to whom an asset or right is assigned.

**assignment (assign)**
The transfer of ownership of an item from one person to another.

**assignment form/notice**
See *allocation notice*.

**assignor**
A person who assigns an asset or right to another party.

### Association of Independent Financial Advisers (AIFA) [UK]
The industry body for independent financial advisers, its objectives are to promote the views and needs of IFAs to government and regulators, and to promote value of independent advice to the public.

### Association of Investment Companies (AIC) [UK]
A trade organisation for the closed-ended investment company industry, representing investment trusts, venture capital trusts and other similar organisationas. It was formed in 1932 as the Association of Investment Trust Companies, and changed its name in 2006. Its main aims are the protection and promotion of the interests of its members and their shareholders.

### Association of Private Client Investment Managers and Stockbrokers (APCIMS) [UK]
An association formed in 1990 to represent the interests of stockbroking and investment management firms which specialise in the provision of services for private investors (also known as private clients). Members are regulated by the Financial Services Authority (FSA).

### Association of Unit Trusts and Investment Funds (AUTIF) [UK]
A trade association formed in 1959 to represent the interests of its members and known then as the Unit Trust Association. The Association was renamed AUTIF in April 1993.
Its main objectives are improving the regulatory environment, increasing public awareness and providing information and assistance to its members.

### assurance [UK]
In the UK the term 'assurance' tends to be used where *insurance* is taken out against something which will inevitably occur, an example being death and thus *life assurance*. The term 'insurance' is used when insuring against an event which may occur such as damage to a motor vehicle. See *endowment assurance* and *insurance*.

### assured
In the UK the assured is a person (or persons) who has entered into a *life assurance* contract with a life office and is the policyholder. The person on whose life the policy is taken out is known as the *life assured*. The assured and the life assured are often the same person but not always. In the USA the expression 'insured' is used. In life insurance, the insured is the person (or persons) who has entered into a contract and on whose life the policy is written. On the death of the insured the face amount of the policy passes to the beneficiary.

### ATM card
A plastic card enabling the holder to access an *automated teller machine* to obtain cash and statements.

### at the money
A situation where the *exercise price* of a call/put option approximates to the current market price of the *underlying instrument*.

### audit
The official examination of a company's accounts by a qualified accountant external to the company.

### auditor
A person appointed by a company to perform an audit.

## authorised share capital [UK]
The total amount of capital (money) a company is authorised to raise by reference to its articles and memorandum of association.

## authorized stock [USA]
The total number of shares which a corporation may issue by reference to its *articles of incorporation*.

## authorised unit trust [UK]
A *unit trust* which has applied for and received approval from the *Financial Services Authority (FSA)* as being suitable for promotion in the UK. Such unit trusts are exempt from tax on capital gains within the trust.

## automated pit trading
A computer based trading system operating in *futures* markets incorporating the features of *open outcry* transactions.

## automated teller machine (ATM)
Also known as cash dispenser. A computerised self service machine allowing the holder of an ATM card and authorised personal identification number (PIN) to obtain cash and statements etc.

## automobile insurance [USA]
*Insurance* taken out by the *insured* for cover against automobile damage or loss such as collision or theft and for cover against injuries to persons, damage to property and medical expenses. In the UK this is known as *motor insurance*.

## averaging
A term used to describe additional purchases of shares in a company or companies when the price has fallen which has the effect of lowering the average buying price.

### back end load [USA]
A charge imposed when redeeming shares in *mutual funds* to discourage withdrawals. These charges often reduce to zero over a period of time, typically five years. Also known as deferred sales charge. In the UK this is known as an *exit charge*.

### back taxes [USA]
Taxes that have not been paid on the due date or were underreported either by accident or by intention on a past tax return. The tax authorities can demand payment of back taxes plus the imposing of penalties.

### back to back loan [UK]
A situation where an investment organisation, such as an *investment trust*, deposits sterling with a UK bank which subsequently arranges with a foreign associate bank to lend the equivalent amount of foreign currency to the investment organisation. The purpose of this transaction is to *hedge* against currency fluctuations affecting the portfolio.

### back to back plan [UK]
The combination of a *life assurance* policy and an *annuity* on the same life with the purpose of reducing *inheritance tax*. The *annuitant* seeks to replace capital expended for the annuity by paying premiums on a life policy, the proceeds of which pass to his/her dependants on death and outside the estate.

### backwardation
A *futures* market term where the nearby price of a *commodity* exceeds the *forward price*.

### BACS Limited [UK]
A clearing service for automated payments. Now renamed *VocaLink*.

### balanced mutual fund [USA]
A *mutual fund* which invests in a balance of *common stock*, *bonds* and *preferred stock* with an objective of income provision and some capital appreciation with low risk.

### balance of payments (BOP)
A country's financial position, with other countries of the world, which is made up of its current account and capital account (or capital movement) over a given period of time. The current account covers the balance of imports and exports. (See *balance of trade*). The capital account covers the difference between capital invested in other countries and by other countries.

### balance of trade (BOT)
The difference between exports and imports of visible (for example, manufactured goods) and invisible (for example, insurance) items over a given period of time.

### balance sheet
A statement showing the *assets*, *liabilities* and *capital* of a company enabling its financial status to be observed at a particular time.

### Baltic Exchange
A self regulated London exchange serving world wide interests. It is the world's premier maritime market for ship

***balloon***

chartering and sale and purchase. The Exchange publishes a range of market information and freight derivatives price settlements.

**balloon [USA]**
The final payment on a loan which is significantly larger than those preceding it.

**band earnings [UK]**
Pay between the *lower earnings limit* and *upper earnings limit* which is used to determine *National Insurance Contributions*.

**bank**
An institution organised to receiving money from individuals, corporations, organisations etc. and making payments on their behalf and to make profit for itself. It may arrange loans for both individuals and companies and charges interest during the repayment period. Money deposited with a bank may also itself earn interest. In the USA, banks are regulated under the *Federal Reserve System*. Banks operating in the UK, formerly regulated by the Bank of England, are now authorised and regulated by the *Financial Services Authority*.

**bank credit [USA]**
The maximum credit an individual may secure from his/her bank.

**bank giro credit [UK]**
A system operated by the clearing banks in which a paper slip/document instructs a bank branch to credit a sum of money to a specified account at that branch.

**bank insurance fund [USA]**
A fund held by a section of the *Federal Deposit Insurance Corporation* as deposit insurance for banks excluding *thrifts*.

**bank line [USA]**
A moral, rather than a contractual commitment by a bank to provide a loan to a borrower up to a stated total amount over a stated period, typically one year. Because a bank line is not a legal commitment, it is not usual to for a commitment fee to be charged. However it is often necessary to keep compensating balances on deposit, typically 10% of the bank line plus an additional 10% of actual borrowings. Where customers are officially notified in respect of a line the term is advised line or confirmed line. In cases where the bank sets an internal guide and the customer is not notified the term is guidance line. Bank line is also known as a line of credit.

**Bank of England**
The central bank of the United Kingdom working in conjunction with the government as its banker and maintaining the integrity and value of the nation's currency. It ensures the stability and promotes the efficiency and competitiveness of the financial system and has operational responsibility for setting interest rates in order to achieve the government's inflation target. The Bank also manages the government's foreign currency borrowing programme, is responsible for setting the level of interest rates as the primary means of achieving the government's inflation targets, and controls the design, production and issue of banknotes in England and Wales. Apart from the government, its other main customers include the commercial banks and foreign central banks. The Bank is sometimes known as 'The Old Lady of Threadneedle Street'.

### bank statement
A document, issued by a bank to its customers, listing details of debit and credit transactions over a given period with a resultant balance of the account. These statements are issued to cover a range of accounts including current accounts, loan accounts and deposit accounts etc.

### Bankers Automated Clearing Services
See *BACS Limited*.

### banker's draft
In situations where a person owes money (particularly a large amount) to another who is not prepared to accept a personal cheque, the former can make the cheque payable to his/her bank. The bank in turn draws a cheque on itself (the banker's draft) which is submitted to the person to whom the sum is owed, which transaction is undisputed.

### banker's reference
A reference sought from a bank by a company or individual regarding the creditworthiness of another company or individual in order to assess whether or not credit trading terms should be offered.

### Banking Ombudsman [UK]
See *Ombudsman*.

### bankruptcy
A situation where an individual is incapable of settling his/her debts and has been served a bankruptcy order by a court.

### bargain
A term used on the *London Stock Exchange* to describe a share purchase or sale. No special price is implied.

## barter
An exchange of products or services between individuals without the involvement of money.

## base metals
The main industrial non-ferrous metals excluding precious metals and minor metals. These are copper, primary aluminium, lead, nickel, tin and zinc. See *London Metal Exchange*.

## base rate [UK]
The lowest rate at which a bank will charge interest. Typically, depending on the circumstances of the borrower, the bank will charge at some level above base rate. (for example, where base rate is 7% and interest charged is 9%, then it is said that interest is 2% above base rate and will continue at this difference as base rates vary unless renegotiated by the borrower.) The USA equivalent is *prime rate*. The Bank of England's *repo rate* is often referred to as its base rate.

## Basel Accord
An agreement on the capital requirements for banks and other deposit-taking institutions was made in Basel in 1988 under the auspices of the Bank for International Settlements. This was expanded and updated in 2007 by a new agreement commonly known as Basel II.

## basic pension [UK]
The basic state pension funded by an individual's *National Insurance Contributions*. The rate at which it is paid is dependent on the person's contributions record over his/her working life.

## basic rate tax
The main rate of *income tax* in the UK, currently 20% on the first £37,400 of taxable income (2009/10 tax year). Above that, a higher rate (40%) applies.

### basic sum assured [UK]
A term used in conjunction with policies such as *low cost endowment assurance*. Such policies operate on a 'with profits' basis and often in conjunction with repaying a loan such as a *mortgage*. In the event of death during the term, a *guaranteed death benefit* repays the loan. However, to guarantee to pay the entire loan at maturity would incur very high premiums. Accordingly, a policy with lower premiums guarantees to repay only a proportion of the loan amount at maturity (the basic sum assured). The expectancy then is that the balance will be repaid by way of *reversionary* and (possibly) *terminal bonuses*.

### basis
The difference between the price of a *futures* contract and the spot or cash price. The item being traded may be a *commodity* or a financial instrument.

### bear
An investor who believes share prices are going to fall. He/she therefore sells shares in anticipation of buying them back at a lower price.

### bear market
A market in which share prices are falling and in which a *bear* would profit.

### bear spread
A strategy in *options* trading in which an option is purchased at an *exercise price* above that of the *underlying instrument* and simultaneously an option is sold at an exercise price below that of the underlying instrument, both with reference to the same expiry month. This applies to either *call options* or *put options*.

## bearer bond

A bond which does not record its owner's name. Possession of the bond certificate is therefore the only proof of ownership. Dividends are claimed by submitting a detachable coupon to the paying agent.

## bearer stocks/shares

Stocks or shares which do not record owner's names and issued by companies which do not keep a register of ownership. Possession of the certificate is therefore the only proof of ownership.

## bed and breakfast [UK]

A former practice of selling shares and their re-purchase the following day. This was based on the assumption it was unlikely that a share price would change very much from its afternoon value to the following morning. The purpose was to take advantage of *capital gains tax* allowance. This strategy could be used to establish 1) a capital loss which could be offset against other gains or 2) a capital gain to lessen future liabilities. The March 1998 Budget effectively ended bed and breakfasting by asserting that shares could not be repurchased within 30 days of being sold, for CGT purposes.

## beneficial loan [UK]

A loan made by an employer to an employee on which interest is either not charged or is less than the official rate. The difference between the interest charged and the official rate is taxable.

## beneficial owner

The true owner of a *security* or property which may be registered in another name. In the USA, when stocks are held by a broker in *street name* the true owner is the beneficial owner even though the broker holds title. In the UK the equivalent situation would be shares registered in a *nominee account*.

### beneficiary
1. A person who benefits from a trust set up on his/her behalf.
2. Anyone who benefits from the proceeds of a will.
3. A person who benefits from the proceeds of a life insurance policy.

### Benefits Agency [UK]
An executive agency within the Department for Work and Pensions (DWP). The Benefits Agency is the provider of state pensions, child benefit, industrial injuries, disablement benefit and other social security benefits.

### benefits in kind
These are benefits, excluding salaries, given to employees which include cars and car fuel, medical insurance and gifts etc.

### bequest
The making of a gift by *will*. See *legacy*.

### best advice [UK]
A requirement of the Financial Services Act 1986 that a financial adviser must provide best appropriate advice regarding the most suitable product for a client, having first established a full understanding of his/her financial background. Now superseded by the concept of *suitability*.

### Best's Ratings [USA]
Ratings of financial reliability given by Best's Rating Service to insurance companies with a top rating of A+. This

information is of importance to both buyers of insurance and investors in insurance stocks.

## beta shares [UK]
A term previously given to the shares of *listed companies*, basically second in line to and traded with less activity than *alpha shares* on the *London Stock Exchange*, along with *gamma* and *delta shares*. These terms were replaced by the *normal market size* classification in January 1991.

## beta value
A measurement of the movement of the price of a particular stock/share compared with the movement of the market as a whole. For example a stock with a beta value of one would be expected to move in line with an index such as the *Standard and Poor's Composite Index (S&P 500)* or the *FTSE 100 Index*. Beta values of less than one would imply less risk but less chance of gain. Beta values of greater than one imply more risk but more chance of gain.

## bid
The price which a purchaser is prepared to pay for an item.

## bid price
The price at which a *market maker* will buy a security (stocks, shares, bonds etc) or a management company will buy back units in a *unit trust* from investors. See *offer price*.

## bid and asked [USA]
Bid is the highest price an investor is prepared to pay for a security. Asked is the lowest price a seller is prepared to accept.

## bid asked spread [USA]
The difference between the *bid price* and asked price for a security. The two terms make up a *quotation*.

## bid/offer spread [UK]
The difference between the *bid price* and the *offer price* for shares and for units in a *unit trust*. It includes an allowance for the *initial charge* if there is one plus dealing costs.

## Big Bang
A term referring to major operational changes on the *London Stock Exchange* made on 27th October 1986. These included the introduction of *market makers* to combine the functions of stockbrokers and stockjobbers and the ending of fixed commissions.

## Big Board
A popular name for the *New York Stock Exchange*.

## billing cycle [USA]
The time between periodic billings for goods and services, typically one month.

## bill of exchange (BE)
An order in writing by one person to another to pay a specified sum to a specified person or bearer on a particular date. The person making the order or drawing the bill is known as the drawer. The person to whom the bill is addressed is the drawee (for example a bank). The person to whom the bill is payable is the payee.

## bill of sale
A formal document for the transference of title to goods from the seller to buyer.

## bi-weekly mortgage loan [USA]
A *mortgage* whereby the borrower makes a half monthly payment every two weeks instead of the usual 12 monthly payments. This arrangement results in 26 half monthly

payments per year and a significant reduction in interest since an extra monthly payment is made, also an early repayment of the loan.

**black knight**
A company (or person) making an unwanted, hostile bid for another company. See grey knight. See white knight.

**Black Monday**
Monday 19th October 1987 when stockmarket values around the world fell heavily triggered by a large fall in the ***Dow Jones Industrial Average*** in the USA.

**blue chip**
The stocks or shares of larger and well established corporations/companies which are sound and highly regarded for their quality products and their potential to pay dividends.

**bona fide**
A term meaning 'in good faith'. For example a person entering into an insurance contract is required to divulge all pertinent information in good faith. Failure to do so could result in breach of the contract and thus making it void. See ***uberrimae fidei***.

**bond**
A fixed interest security issued by governments and corporations/companies where guarantees are given to repay the capital and interest is paid at a rate as specified on the bond or policy document.

**bond anticipation note (BAN) [USA]**
A short term municipal or state note which is repaid from the proceeds of a forthcoming issue.

### bond discount
The difference between a bond's *face value* and the *market price*. If the market price is higher than the face value, the difference is known as the bond premium. When interest rates rise, it is usual for bond prices to fall and when interest rates fall it is usual for bond prices to increase.

### bond mutual fund [USA]
A *mutual fund* which invests in bonds which may be government, municipal or corporate etc.

### bond rating [USA]
Ratings by various rating services regarding the likelihood of default by a bond issuer. These include Standard and Poor's and Moody's. Ratings range from AAA (highly regarded) to D (default).

### bond yield
The return to an investor on the capital investment in a bond, that is, the interest paid expressed as a percentage of capital outlay. Where bonds are traded on a stock exchange, the yield will be dependent on the current purchase price and thus will vary. As the price of a bond falls, so the yield increases and vice versa.

### bonus [USA]
A sum paid by a life insurance company to the *insured* based on investment proceeds.
[UK] An additional sum paid on a *with profits* assurance contract to policyholders. The amount is dependent on the profits of the assurance company. *Reversionary bonuses* are usually added annually whilst a *terminal bonus* may be payable at maturity or in the event of the death of the *life assured*.

## bonus declaration [UK]
The declaration by a life company as to the rate of bonuses on a *with profits* policy. *Reversionary bonuses* are normally paid annually and could typically be in the region of 2% to 5%. *Terminal bonuses* (payable at maturity or prior death) tend to vary much more but could vary from say 10% to 100% at maturity depending on the term of the policy, for example ten and twenty five year terms.

## bonus issue
See *scrip issue*.

## book
A record maintained by a trading specialist of buy and sell orders for a given security.

## book value
The value of an asset as entered in an organisation's *books of account*.

## books of account
The books in which the transactions of a business are recorded.

## bought deal
The purchase of new shares by an underwriter who subsequently attempts to resell to the market for a profit.

## bourse
A French or continental European stock exchange.

## break even
The level of a company's sales at which neither a profit nor a loss is made.

**break up value**
The value of a company's assets sold individually if the company is unable to continue trading.

**Bretton Woods Agreement**
An agreement made in Bretton Woods, USA in 1944 which established a post-war fixed currency rate between countries and subsequently the International Monetary Fund (IMF). The fixed exchange rate functioned until the early 1970s when it was replaced by a floating exchange rate.

**bridge loan (bridging loan)**
A short term loan, typically made by a bank to a customer in anticipation of a long term loan. For example, a bridge loan would be used to purchase a property prior to the completion of the sale of an existing property.

**broad money [UK]**
See *money supply*.

**broker**
A business *agent* with specialist knowledge of a market, for example, *stockbroker* and *insurance broker*. Brokers offer advice to clients and are either paid by a fixed fee or by commission.

**brokerage fee**
Commission or fees charged by a broker for conducting transactions for its clients.

**budget account**
A bank account set up to control a person's regular expenditure. The account would typically include the payment of such items as mortgage, utilities, telephone and other similar items. Annual expenditure for each item is

divided by 12 and paid into the account monthly. The bills are then paid from the budget account as they become due.

## Building Societies Investor Protection Scheme [UK]
A scheme set up to give limited protection to persons with share and/or deposit accounts in authorised building societies which fail. Now replaced by the *Financial Services Compensation Scheme*.

## building society [UK]
A non profit making deposit-taking institution whose principle purpose is making loans which are secured on residential property and funded substantially by its members. Building societies are regulated by the *Financial Services Authority (FSA)*. See *deposit account* and *share account*.

## buildings insurance [UK]
Insurance which covers the policyholder against certain building losses or damages which may occur. The insurers will usually specify a maximum claim limit (the sum insured) which is the full rebuilding cost of the home. It is the owner's responsibility to ensure the sum insured is correct and to regularly update this cover. See *contents insurance*.

## bull
An investor who believes prices of *shares/commodities* etc are going to rise. He/she is therefore a buyer in anticipation of selling at a higher price. See *bear*.

## bull market
A market in which prices are rising and in which a *bull* would profit. See *bear market*.

## bull spread
A strategy in *options* trading in which an option is purchased at an *exercise price* below that of the *underlying instrument*

and simultaneously an option is sold at an exercise price above that of the underlying instrument, both with reference to the same expiry month. This applies to both *call options* or *put options*.

**bulldog bond**
A bond issued on the UK market by a foreign institution.

**bullion**
Gold or silver in the form of ingots for bulk use.

**bullion coins**
Coins made from gold or silver. They can be easily traded.

**buy-to-let [UK]**
The practice of purchasing residential property with a view to letting it to tenants. The phrase has come to refer specifically to mortgages designed to assist investors without their own capital to enter this market.

**Buyers Guide [UK]**
A document, formerly used by financial advisers to inform prospective clients of the adviser's identity and status. Now replaced by the *client agreement*.

**bylaws [USA]**
The rules under which a corporation's internal management operates. They include details such as election of directors, duties of officers and how share transfers can be conducted. See *articles of incorporation*.

## cafeteria employee benefit plan [USA]
A plan enabling employees to choose from a variety of benefits, depending on their own particular circumstances. Young employees for example will have different requirements from those of older employees.

## call [USA]
The redeeming of a *bond* by an issuer before its maturity date.
[UK]
1. A demand by a company to shareholders to pay a further instalment on partly paid shares.
2. A demand by a bank for the full repayment of a loan when the borrower has failed to meet his/her obligations under the terms of the loan agreement.

## call date
[USA] The date on which a *bond* may be redeemed by the issuer before maturity which may be at par or at a higher value. The difference is known as the call premium.

## call option
An *option* which gives the *holder* the right but not the obligation to purchase a stated quantity of the *underlying instrument* (for example shares, indices, commodities etc) at a specified price on or before a given date. See *put option*.

## call price [USA]
The price at which a *bond* or *preferred stock* can be redeemed by the issuer. The call price will usually be greater than the

par value to compensate the holder for loss of income and ownership. The difference is known as the call premium.

**call provision [USA]**
A provision of a *bond* or *preferred stock* issue, listed in its *indenture* (the formal agreement between the bond issuer and the holder) that allows the issuer to redeem the bond before the maturity date either at par or at a premium to par.

**cancel**
1. To make an agreement void.
2. [USA] The voiding of a buy or sell order.

**cancellation notice [UK]**
A notice which must be given to investors entering into long term insurance contracts informing them they have the right to cancel within 14 days of receipt of the notice.

**cancellation price [UK]**
The lowest possible *bid price* of units in a *unit trust* under *FSA* regulations which is usually lower than the quoted bid price. The cancellation price may be applied in the event of heavy selling.

**capital**
1. The overall assets of an individual less liabilities.
2. Money injected into a company by way of *share capital* and *loan capital* plus *retained earnings*.

**capital allowance [UK]**
A tax allowance which takes account of depreciation of certain types of business assets such as plant and machinery and motor vehicles etc.

**capital assets**
Assets, purchased as a long term investment for generating profit, such as buildings, plant and machinery and fixtures etc.

## capital employed
Capital used to produce profit.

## capital expenditure
A company's expenditure to acquire *capital assets*.

## capital gain
The difference between the selling price of an asset and the buying price.

## capital gains tax (CGT)
A tax imposed on the profits from the sale of assets. In the USA, if the *holding period* of the asset is over one year, tax treatment of any gain is more favourable. In the UK, gains are taxed after taking into consideration an annual capital gains allowance after which a rate of 18% is applied (2009/10). A special 'entrepreneur's rate of 10% (2009/10) applies to the first £1million of cumulative gains arising from the disposal of trading businesses.

## capital gearing
See *gearing*.

## capital growth
Capital assets, for example shares or a house, which increase in value.

## capital movement
See *balance of payments*.

## capital shares [USA]
Shares which entitle the holder to receive the capital appreciation from a *dual purpose fund*. The other type of shares in such a fund are *income shares* which receive the fund's income. In the UK this type of fund is called a *split capital investment trust*.

## capital structure

**[UK]**
1. Shares which entitle the holder to receive the capital appreciation from the portfolio of a split capital investment trust.
2. Shares whose value to an investor are expected to be by way of significant share price increase rather than payment of income.

### capital structure [USA]
The components which form a corporation's capital that is, *common stock*, *long term debt* and *preferred stock*.
**[UK]** The components which together form a company's capital. These include *ordinary shares*, *preference shares*, *debentures* and *loan stock*.

### capitalisation
1. The injection of capital into a company.
2. See *capital structure*.
3. The reserves of a company which are converted into additional shares for shareholders.

### capitalisation issue
See *scrip issue*.

### car benefit [UK]
Where a company provides an employee or director with a company motor car which is used privately in addition to company business, a tax liability may arise which will depend on a number of factors including salary and motor car details such as cost and level of carbon dioxide emissions.

### carat
A measurement unit defining the purity of gold. Pure gold is 24 carat, whilst 18 carat gold comprises 18/24 gold and 6/24 alloy.

## cash flow

**carry forward and carry back [UK]**
Formerly systems under which personal pension holders could utilise tax relief from earlier tax years. Abolished in 2001 and 2006 respectively.

**cash**
Money, in the form of notes and coins, which constitutes payment for goods at the time of purchase.

**cash and carry**
An *arbitrage* transaction applied on a *futures* market where the cash or *spot price* of for example, a *commodity* is less than the *futures contract* price. Under these circumstances a purchase of the cash commodity with borrowed money and the simultaneous sale of the futures contract can provide a profit.

**cash card**
See *ATM card*.

**cash dividend [USA]**
A payment of a proportion of a corporation's profits to shareholders in the form of cash. An alternative form of payment is by way of stock, that is, a *stock dividend*. In the UK cash dividends are known simply as dividends. When a company pays a dividend in the form of shares it is sometimes known as a *scrip dividend*.

**cash dispenser**
See *automated teller machine*.

**cash flow**
The measure of cash received and cash spent by a company, institution or individual.

### cash market
An expression used to describe the market in the *underlying instrument* (for example, shares, indices, commodities, etc.) on which a *futures* or *options* contract is based. Also known as *spot* or *physical* market. In a cash market the commodity or financial instrument is transferred from seller to buyer.

### cash settlement
1. Deals on an exchange where investors are obliged to settle immediately rather than on account.
2. An expression used in *futures* and *options* trading which applies when physical delivery is impractical and contracts are settled by attaching a monetary value.

### cash surrender value [USA]
The value of funds returnable to the *insured* from the *insurer* upon the surrender of a *cash value life insurance* policy.

### cash value life insurance [USA]
A *life insurance* policy which pays a benefit on the death of the *insured* but which also provides a savings element where benefits are payable before death.

### casualty insurance [USA]
Insurance which gives protection to a business or homeowner against property loss, damage and injury to a third party.

### caveat emptor
Latin for 'let the buyer beware'. This implies a buyer must ensure that goods about to be purchased are free from defects and that he/she bears the risk.

### Central Register [UK]
Now known as the FSA Register, this online database enables the public to check whether a financial services

### chargeable event certificate

firm is authorised. Information listed includes the name, address and telephone number of each firm's main place of business.

### certificate of deduction of tax [UK]
A certificate, issued by a building society or bank (in accordance with Section 352 of the Income and Corporation Taxes Act 1988) to its customers with interest bearing accounts, in which gross interest, tax deducted and net interest are depicted.

### certificate of deposit
A certificate, issued by a bank to a depositor, indicating a sum of money has been deposited for a specified term and on which interest is paid.

### charge card
A plastic payment card enabling the holder to obtain goods and services without the requirement to pay cash. Accounts are normally submitted to the card holder monthly and must be settled in full. In addition to obtaining goods, the charge card can be used to obtain cash. Examples of charge cards are *American Express* and *Diners Club*. See also *credit card* and *debit card*.

### chargeable event [UK]
A transaction which leads to a *chargeable gain* and which in turn promotes the issuing of a *chargeable event certificate*. For example the sale of an investment bond with a life company which results in a gain will be classed as a chargeable event.

### chargeable event certificate [UK]
A certificate issued on the occurrence of a *chargeable event*. Details listed include the amount of the gain, number of years

## chargeable gain

over which the gain has occurred, the date the transaction took place and that the certificate should be sent to the Tax Office to establish if a higher rate tax liability exists. Proceeds are free from basic rate tax liability.

### chargeable gain [UK]
The amount of a gain which may incur a tax liability.

### charity
An organisation whose aim is to provide help for the needy, or contribute to other worthy causes. Charities which are registered with the appropriate authority (in the UK, the Charity Commission) can receive legacies from a deceased person's estate free of inheritance tax.

### charitable trust
A trust which has been registered with the appropriate authority and which enjoys income tax advantages.

### chartist
An analyst who uses graphs relating to past performance of securities etc. to anticipate future trends.

### chattels
A term used in wills which refers to the personal possessions of the maker of the *will*. Such items would typically be jewellery, furniture, books, tools and private motor cars etc.

### check [USA] cheque [UK]
A printed form on which a written order is given to a person's or company's bank to pay a specific sum to a named recipient or bearer.

### check card [USA] cheque card [UK]
A card, issued by a bank (or a building society in the UK), which guarantees the payment of a check to the recipient

and which supports a check for obtaining cash, both up to a stated value.

### check clearing [USA] cheque clearing [UK]
A system which enables checks to be transmitted between banks (and between branches) in order to transfer funds.

### checking account [USA] cheque account [UK]
An account, with a bank (or additionally a *building society* in the UK) into which deposits are made and from which payments are made by check. See also *deposit account*. Generally referred to in the UK as a *current account*

### Chicago Climate Exchange
A greenhouse gas reduction and trading system for emission sources and offset projects.

### child deferred endowment [UK]
An *endowment assurance*, on the life of a child, which can be taken as cash at *maturity* or converted to a *full endowment* or *whole life assurance*.

### Child Trust Fund [UK]
A government-assisted long-term tax-free savings scheme for children from birth to age 18. The government adds £250 at birth and at age 7. Parents or others can add up to £1,200 per year.

### Citizens Advice [UK]
An organisation, represented in many towns in the UK, where the public can obtain free advice on an extensive range of civil matters including social security, consumer matters such as loans and rental arrears, employment, housing matters such as mortgage and rent arrears, legal matters such as legal aid, family matters, taxation and many other subjects.

## claim
A demand by the *insured* for a benefit to be paid by the insurers under the conditions of the policy.

## Class 1, 2, 3 and 4 National Insurance Contributions [UK]
See *National Insurance Contributions*.

## clawback [UK]
Where a life company advances *indemnity commission* to an agent, the company does so on the understanding it will be entitled to take back some or all (clawback) such commission if the relevant policy is cancelled within a given period.

## clearing
1. The process of moving payments between accounts from different banks or branches.
2. [UK] A term used on *futures* and *options* exchanges which refers to the process of registration, settlement and provision of a guarantee of exchange traded transactions.

## clearing corporation [USA], clearing house [UK]
An independent organisation, appointed by an exchange, which guarantees securities transactions.

## client agreement
A document issued by an adviser/broker to a client outlining the basis of the relationship and the services for which the adviser/broker is authorised. It is a legal requirement in the UK, whether advisers are independent or tied agents, that a client agreement be given to a prospective client (*prospect*) prior to any product discussions.

## close market [USA]
A securities market in which the difference between bid and offer prices is narrow and which depicts high volume trading.

## close out
A *futures* transaction where an equal and opposite trade closes an *open position*. This leaves a trader with what is known as a zero net position.

## closed corporation [USA]
A corporation in which publicly held shares are owned by only a few individuals and not usually available for trading.

## closed end fund
A fund which has a fixed number of shares which are normally be traded on a stock exchange where prices are affected by supply and demand. See *open end fund*.

## closely held corporation [USA]
A corporation with only a small number of shareholders. Although a public company, shares would not normally be available for trading.

## closing purchase
The purchase of an *option*, by a *writer*, which has the same terms as an option which has previously been sold. This transaction terminates his/her obligations as a writer.

## closing range
A *futures* expression which refers to a range of closely allied prices at which transactions were conducted at the close of a trading day.

### closing sale
The sale of an *option*, by a *holder*, identical to the option which is held. This transaction terminates his/her rights as a holder.

### codicil
A document on which changes or additions are made to an existing signed will. The will and the codicil must be read in conjunction with one another.

### cold calling
An approach by a salesperson to a prospect (prospective buyer) either by telephone or in person where no previous contact has been made. In the UK, when cold calling in respect of life assurance, pensions and unit trusts, a code of practice must be followed by the salesperson which includes the declaration of the name of the caller and his/her company and the purpose of the call etc.

### collateral
An asset pledged as a guarantee to a lender until a loan is repaid. An example is a life insurance policy which has acquired a *cash surrender value* equal or greater in value to the loan amount.

### collecting branch
A banking term which refers to the branch which accepts cheques to be credited to its customers' accounts and subsequently obtains the proceeds from the issuing banks, usually by a clearing arrangement.

### COMEX
Formerly an abbreviation for the Commodity Exchange in New York and now a division of the *New York Mercantile Exchange* after its merger with NYMEX. It is the main US

market for metals *futures* and *options* trading in copper, gold and silver.

**commercial bank [UK]**
A bank, such as Barclays, Lloyds, which provides services to companies and individuals in the form of current, deposit and loan accounts plus a variety of other financial services including mortgages, insurance and financial planning etc. Also commonly known as 'High Street' banks.

**commercial mortgage**
A *mortgage* on a non residential building within which a business operates.

**commercial paper**
A short term *note* issued by banks and corporations with a range of maturities typically from 30 days to 270 days.

**commission**
Payment made to an *agent* for his/her part in the sale of products to a client or customer. The payment is invariably made to the agent by his/her *principal*, that is, the originator of the product.

**commodity (commodities)**
Basic raw materials and foodstuffs such as metals, petroleum, coffee, grain etc. An article of trade as opposed to a service. Commodities are traded on a commodity exchange. In the USA, commodities of various types are traded on a number of exchanges including the Chicago Board of Trade, Chicago Mercantile Exchange, Kansas City Board of Trade and Mid America Commodity Exchange. In the UK, commodities are traded on the London Metal Exchange, the International Petroleum Exchange and NYSE Liffe, the international derivatives exchange of NYSE Euronext.

### commodity broker
A broker who deals in *commodities* in a commodities market.

### common stock [USA]
A share in a public or private company where the holder is an owner in the company. He/she is entitled to vote on the election of directors and to receive a dividend in relation to the extent of his/her stock holding. Holders of common stock will also seek to enhance the capital value of their investment by way of stock price increase over the longer term. In the event of the company being wound up holders of common stock are the last in line to be paid. Similar to an ordinary share in the UK.

### common stock fund [USA]
A *mutual fund* which invests solely in common stocks of companies.

### community charge [UK]
A charge, levied on all adult citizens in the UK, which replaced the previous rates system for council finance. The charge was unpopular and was subsequently replaced by the *council tax* in 1993.

### community property [USA]
Property owned by a married couple and held jointly.

### commutation [UK]
A term used to describe a person's right to convert part of his/her *pension* fund into cash (tax free) at retirement age at the expense of a reduced pension. See *occupational pension scheme* and *personal pension plan*.

**Companies House [UK]**
See *Registrar of Companies*.

**company doctor**
A business executive specializing in rectifying the problems of companies in difficulties.

**company pension**
See *occupational pension scheme*.

**company representative (tied agent) [UK]**
The representative of a particular company, authorised to give *financial advice* on products such as *life assurance*, *pensions* and *unit trusts*. Such a representative may recommend products from that company only (or, in the case of multi-tie, from a limited range of specified providers). Under the *Financial Services and Markets Act 2000* all financial advisers must declare to the client whether they are a company representative/tied agent or *independent financial adviser (IFA)* and they must present to the client a *client agreement* prior to any product discussions.

**compensating balance [USA]**
The balance required to be kept on deposit at a bank by a borrower when taking out a loan. Should the borrower fail to repay the loan either in full or in part, this balance would be forfeited. Compensating balances are typically 10% of the loan amount.

**Competition Commission [UK]**
An independent public body that investigates the suitability of acquisitions and mergers. It vetoed a proposed merger between Lloyds TSB Bank and Abbey National Bank in 2001, believing that it would materially reduce competition and innovation in the provision of banking services.

### compliance [USA]
Procedures adopted by stock exchanges to oversee trading to ensure compliance with the *Securities and Exchange Commission* rules.
[UK] Procedures that must be adopted by financial services providers, their representatives and independent intermediaries, as a result of the *Financial Services and Markets Act 2000*. Companies each appoint a compliance officer to ensure that compliance procedures are followed.

### compound interest
Interest, which is earned on the principal over a given period (for example, one year), is added to the principal and in subsequent periods the principal plus interest earn further interest.
For example: Principal = $1,000. Compound interest paid annually at 5%
At end of first year, principal + interest= $1,000.00 + $50.00 = $1,050.00
At end of second year, (principal + interest) + interest = $1,050.00 + $52.50 = $1,102.50

### compound reversionary bonus [UK]
A *with profits* life assurance bonus, normally added annually to the policy, which is based on the profits of the life company's investments. The compound reversionary bonus is normally calculated on the *sum assured* (or *basic sum assured*) plus bonuses to date and is payable at the maturity of the policy or prior death. Once declared, reversionary bonuses are guaranteed.

### comprehensive insurance
A term used to describe an insurance policy in which a wide range of risks are covered, an example being comprehensive motor insurance.

**compulsory purchase annuity**
See *annuity*.

**Confederation of British Industry (CBI)**
An independent non-profit making, non party political organisation which represents the interests of over 200,000 direct and indirect member companies in the UK. The CBI was founded in 1965 by the merging of the Federation of British Industries, the British Employers' Confederation and the National Association of British Manufacturers.
Finance is provided by members' subscriptions and a range of other commercial activities including conferences and publications and the membership includes companies of all sizes from all sectors of industry and commerce. The organisation's objective is to develop the conditions necessary for UK businesses to be competitive and to prosper. Close liaison is maintained with the UK government regarding its members' views and increasingly with European Union bodies.

**conglomerate**
A company which owns a number of other companies with widely diversified activities.

**consideration**
Something of value given by one party to another in return for entering into a contract.
[UK] The money value of a *London Stock Exchange* transaction (the value of the sale of a security) excluding costs such as charges and *stamp duty* etc.

**consols**
See *irredeemable stocks*.

### constant dollar plan [USA]
A plan which enables investors to accumulate shares in stock or a *mutual fund* by purchasing on a regular basis (for example monthly) with a fixed dollar amount. When the price is low, more shares will be purchased and fewer when the price is high. Also known as dollar cost averaging. Known as pound cost averaging in the UK.

### Consumer Credit Act [UK]
The legislation that controls the supply of most forms of credit in the UK apart from mortgages. Suppliers of credit must be licensed by the Office of Fair Trading.

### consumer durables
A product such as an automobile or appliance whose life expectancy is at least three years.

### consumer price index (CPI)
An index which tracks the prices of a variety of goods purchased by an average consumer. The goods typically include food, clothing, utilities and in the USA medical care. Also known as the cost of living index which is used as a reference for wage increases and other similar inflation prone items. In the UK the CPI is based on a formula used in the eurozone of the EU and is used to set the government's inflation target. A different measure, the *retail price index* (RPI) is used for calculating inflation-linked state pensions and other benefits.

### contango
A situation in *futures* trading where the future delivery price is greater than the cash or nearby price.

### contents insurance [UK]
Insurance which gives cover in respect of the contents of a home. This includes damage, theft or loss to items such as

carpets, furniture, freezer contents, jewellery and cash etc. It is usual for the insurers to specify a maximum claim limit for each section of items covered. This information is listed on the policy schedule issued by the insurers. Contents insurance can be linked with *buildings insurance* in a combined policy provided by a single company. See *household insurance*.

### contingent assurance [UK]
*Life assurance* where payment of the *sum assured* depends on an event or events additional to the death of the *life assured*. For example the policy may specify the prior death of the spouse of the life assured.

### contingent liabilities
Liabilities (debts) that may or may not be incurred by a company and which depend on the outcome of say a forthcoming event such as a court case. These are recorded in a company's accounts as contingent liabilities.

### contra
An entry made into an account or statement to nullify a previous entry.

### contract
1. A legal agreement between two or more persons.
2. [UK] The minimum amount of a *commodity* or financial instrument in which trading may take place. Also known as a lot.

### contract month
The specified month to which a *futures* or *options* contract refers. This is the month when the specified instrument is delivered in exchange for *cash settlement*.

### contract note
A confirming note, containing details of a stock exchange deal, which is sent from a member firm to its client. The details include the date and time of deal, title of the security, price, consideration (the money value of the transaction) stamp duty (if applicable) and commission etc.

### contract of insurance
A contract between an insurer and the insured. The insurer agrees to pay money to the insured upon the occasion of given events in return for a single premium or regular premiums.

### contracting out [UK]
A term which refers to contracting out of *S2P (Second State Pension)*. A person can contract out by joining an employer's pension scheme which itself is contracted out or through an *appropriate personal pension plan*. The result of making this choice is that the person's S2P pension will be reduced at retirement but there will instead be the proceeds from the alternative pension plan selected.

### contributions waiver benefit
See *waiver of premium*.

### convergence
The movement of a *futures* price towards that of the *underlying instrument* as the contract date approaches.

### conversion terms
1. The terms which apply when convertible loan stock, for example, a *bond* or a *debenture*, are converted into *ordinary shares* or *preference shares*. These would include the price and date of conversion which are fixed at the issue date.

2. The terms which apply when a *warrant* is converted into shares. These would include the exercise price, the date or period of conversion and the number of shares (normally one per warrant) which the warrant holder would be entitled to purchase.

### convertible [USA]
*A bond* or *preferred stock* which can be converted into *common stock* at a given price.
[UK] A bond or *debenture* which may be converted into *ordinary shares* or *preference shares* at a given price at a future date.

### convertible term insurance [USA]
*Term life insurance* which can be converted into *cash value insurance*. In the UK the equivalent (convertible term assurance) is conversion of *term assurance* into *endowment assurance*.

### conveyancing [UK]
The business of the legal transfer of real *property* from one owner to another.

### cooling off period [UK]
The 14 day period during which a new policyholder can cancel an insurance/assurance policy. This is referred to in the *cancellation notice* which must be sent to persons entering into long term policies. The 14 day period starts from receipt of the cancellation notice.

### cooperative
A business owned and operated by its members.

### corporate bond
A debt security issued by a company. The par value, usually $1,000 is repayable at maturity. Interest is payable at regular

intervals throughout the life of the bond. Corporate bonds are tradeable on major stock exchanges.

**corporation tax [UK]**
A tax payable by a company on its profits.

**cost basis**
The cost price of an asset used to establish *capital gains tax* liability.

**cost of sales**
The cost to a company of producing goods. Similarly with a retailer or distributor type business, cost of sales is the cost of purchasing goods prior to their resale.

**council tax [UK]**
A local taxation system which was introduced in 1993 to replace the community charge (poll tax). The tax is based on the property value and the assumption that there are two or more adults in residence (aged over 18). There are eight bands of property values (A to H) and the tax incurred by each dwelling increases in increments from band A to band H. There is no further charge if there are more than two persons resident but if the dwelling is only occupied by one individual, the bill will receive a discount.

**coupon**
The rate of interest paid by the issuer of a bond until maturity.

**coupon bond**
See *bearer bond*.

**court of protection [UK]**
A office of the Supreme Court whose function is to manage and administer the property and affairs of persons who,

through mental disorder, are incapable of managing their own financial affairs.

**covenant**
A formal agreement made in a *deed*.

**cover [USA]**
The net asset value underlying a bond or stock.
**[UK]**
1. The ratio between a company's net profit after tax and the dividend paid to its shareholders. For example: Net profit after tax (earnings) = £700,000.00 Dividend paid = £300,000.00
The cover is £700,000.00 / £300,000.00 = 2.33 times.
Cover indicates a company's capability to continue its dividend payment and can also be viewed as its commitment to investment for future growth. In the USA the reverse ratio is used, that is, dividend payment divided by net earnings, known as *dividend payout ratio*. This gives the percentage of earnings paid to shareholders.
2. The details of insurance provided by an insurance company to the policyholder.

**credit**
1. A sum of money entered into a bank or financial institution account thereby improving the balance.
2. Included in the trading terms between companies, credit is the value of goods which one company will supply to another before payment is necessary.

**credit bureau**
An agency which accumulates credit information relative to the credit reliability of consumers and subsequently makes such information available at a fee to companies offering credit terms.

### credit card
A plastic payment card which allows the owner to obtain goods and services without the requirement to pay cash and on credit terms. Transactions during a month are totalled and presented to the card holder for settlement on a monthly basis. Alternatively a percentage of the outstanding amount can be paid and the balance extended to the next month and so on. This will normally incur a much higher annual rate of interest than usual, for example, 2% per month being equivalent to an *annual percentage rate* of 26.82%. In addition to obtaining goods, the credit card can be used to obtain cash. See also *charge card* and *debit card*.

### credit clearing
A system for the distribution of bank giro credits and other credits between banks to enable funds to be transferred into specified accounts.

### credit control
Methods used by companies to try to ensure their customers pay their accounts/bills within the agreed time period.

### credit note
A note, issued to a person or company when goods are returned by them, which cancels the original invoice. If the invoice has been settled before the goods are returned the credit note will then entitle the holder to alternative goods (or sometimes cash) to the original value.

### credit union
A mutual association formed by persons with a common affiliation such as employees, a union or a religious group in which pooled saving are made. The funds are invested for appreciation and members may borrow at competitive rates.

**creditors**
Persons or companies to whom monies are owed. Thus a company's creditors are those to whom payment is to be made. See *debtors*.

**CREST**
An electronic system of *settlement* for the securities/equities market in the UK and Ireland.
In 1993, the Bank of England initiated the development of CREST to provide faster, cheaper and more efficient paperless settlement. The system went live in 1996, replacing the *TALISMAN* paper system. CREST is owned and operated by *CRESTCo*, part of the *Euroclear* group.

**critical illness cover**
Insurance which covers the insured against specified critical illnesses such as cancer, heart attack and multiple sclerosis etc. In the event that the insured contracts one of the specified illnesses, the insurers would pay a lump sum rather than an income as in the case of *permanent health insurance*.

**Crown [UK]**
A term sometimes used in wills which effectively means HM Treasury. In the event of a deceased person not having made a will (*intestacy*), and there being no traceable living relatives, the proceeds from the estate pass to the Crown.

**cum**
A Latin word meaning 'with'. Thus, for example, cum dividend means with dividend.

**cumulative preference shares [UK]**
When a company fails to pay a dividend, holders of cumulative preference shares are entitled to receive this missed payment when next a dividend is declared. This rule is cumulative

### cumulative preferred stock

and they are also entitled to the current dividend provided sufficient cash is available. These payments receive priority before the holders of ordinary shares.

### cumulative preferred stock [USA]
Preferred stock with dividend payment priority following a missed dividend payment. This amount accumulates with subsequent dividends and when next a dividend is declared no payments can be made to common stockholders until cumulative preferred stockholders have been paid in full.

### curb [USA]
The *American Stock Exchange* which was originally known as the Curb Exchange.

### currency
Cash, bank deposits etc. which circulate in an economy as an accepted means of exchange.

### currency loan
A term used when money is borrowed in a foreign currency.

### currency swap
An arrangement whereby two parties agree to exchange responsibilities for the repayment of two different currency loans. For example a UK company may wish to set up a subsidiary in France and would need a loan in euros. Similarly a French company may wish to take out a loan in pounds sterling. The probability is that the UK company will be able to borrow in pounds sterling at a lower interest rate than in euros. This would also be the case for the French company that is, it would be able to borrow euros at a cheaper interest rate than in sterling. The two companies then exchange loan responsibilities and by so doing each obtains a currency loan at a lower interest rate.

## current yield

**current account**
1. A *balance of payments* account listing transactions other than capital movement.
2. An account listing transactions between trading companies.
3. **[UK]** A bank account which offers a number of facilities including cheque book for debt settlement, deposits, direct debits and where applicable, *overdrafts*. This type of account is normally used for ongoing transactions (for example monthly direct debits and writing of cheques etc.) as opposed to a *deposit account*.

**current assets**
Assets of a company which are regularly turned over including cash, work in progress and debtors (monies owed to the company).

**current income [USA]**
Interest, dividend or other income payments received regularly from an investment source.

**current liabilities**
Debts owed by a company which are due for settlement within 12 months. These include *creditors* (monies owed by the company) and taxes due etc.

**current ratio**
Current assets divided by current liabilities. This ratio gives an indication of a company's capability to pay its debts and as a broad rule should be one or more.

**current yield**
See *yield*.

**Customs and Excise [UK]**
See *Her Majesty's Revenue & Customs*.

**cyclical stock**
Stock in companies whose profits are inclined to move in a cyclical manner, normally in phase with the economy. When prosperous times prevail profits increase but they decrease when the economy declines.

**Daily Official List [UK]**
The daily record of listed securities and price transactions published by the *FSA* in its capacity as the UK Listing Authority (UKLA).

**database**
A structured set of data sorted in various configurations and stored in a computer.

**dated security**
A fixed interest *security* which has a specified date for repayment (redemption date).

**date of record [USA]**
The date by which a shareholder must own shares in order to qualify for a dividend.

**day order**
An order placed with a broker to purchase or sell stock, a *commodity* or financial instrument at specified price limits. If not executed that day the order becomes invalid.

**day trade [USA]**
The purchase and sale of a *security* on the same day.

**days of grace**
Additional days which may be allowed by a company to a *debtor* over and above the due date for payment. For example, a life insurance company may allow days of grace for a policy to be kept in force after the date the *premium* is due for payment.

**deal**
A transaction on a stock exchange by a broker or institution etc.

**dealing**
See *deal*.

**death and superannuation benefit [UK]**
An income tax allowance which can be claimed if certain payments are being made to friendly societies on combined sickness and life insurance policies issued prior to April 2007. The allowance is half of the death benefit part of the premium. Also, relief is obtainable on trade union contributions which relate to superannuation, life insurance or funeral benefits. The allowance is half of the premium. Allowances for superannuation contributions to retirement benefit schemes are usually deducted by the employer before assessing tax on the remaining pay.

**death benefit**
The amount payable by a life insurance company to the *beneficiaries* on the death of the insured (the policyholder). In the US this is the face value of the policy less any outstanding policy loans.

**death duties [UK]**
An old name for *inheritance tax* payable on a deceased person's *estate*. *Estate tax* in the USA.

**death in service**
A life insurance policy which often attaches to a company pension scheme. The member is typically covered for three times his/her salary whilst remaining in the employ of the company and should death occur during this period (death in service), his/her dependants would receive the insured sum free of tax.

## debenture
In the USA an unsecured bond. In the UK a type of loan, taken out by a company, normally to be repaid at a specified future date and with a fixed rate of interest. It is usual for the debenture to be secured against certain of the company's assets, that is, if the company fails to fulfil its interest payments and/or repayment of the loan when due, those assets are liable to be transferred to the lender.

## debit
An outflow of funds from an account with a bank or financial institution. For example: When a person writes a cheque, his/her account will subsequently be debited with the amount.

## debit card
A plastic payment card, issued by a bank or other financial institution, which enables the holder to obtain goods and services without the requirement to pay cash. The debiting procedure commences directly after the transaction which results in the holder's account being debited within a few days. In addition to obtaining goods, the card can be used to obtain cash which results in the holder's account being debited immediately. See also *charge card* and *credit card*.

## debit note
A note, issued to a person or company indicating an amount owed. A more popular method of debiting is by an *invoice.*

## debt
Money owed by an individual or company to another individual or company.

## debt instrument
A promise in writing to repay a debt. For example a bond, bill or note.

### debt security
A *security* such as a bond or note with specified interest, representing a loan which is repayable at some future date.

### debt to equity ratio
The total liabilities of a company divided by stockholders' equity.

### debtor
A person or company owing money to another person or company. A company is therefore owed money by its debtors and those to whom monies are owed are known as its *creditors*.

### declaration date
The date on which a dividend is declared by a company's directors. Once declared the dividend becomes a liability of the company.

### decreasing term life insurance
Life insurance in which the death benefit decreases over the term of the policy although the premiums remain fixed. In the UK this is known as decreasing term assurance.

### deductible
1. An amount (normally fixed) a policyholder is obliged to pay prior to an insurance company paying a claim.
2. [USA] An expense allowed as a deduction from *adjusted gross income* to reduce taxable income. For example, mortgage interest and state and local taxes.

### deduction [USA]
An expense allowed by the *Internal Revenue Service* which is deducted from *adjusted gross income* to establish *taxable income*. These include interest payments and state and local taxes. Known as an allowance in the UK.

## deferment period

[UK] In the UK a deduction is an item which may be additive to income (such as a percentage of the value of a company vehicle). Deductions are subtracted from *allowances* to give tax free pay.

### deed
A document, which legally transfers ownership of property from one party another, more commonly related to real estate.

### deed of covenant [UK]
A legal document, detailed in which is a specified sum of money to be transferred from one individual to another for a specified number of years, in order to save income tax. The individual making the payment deducts tax at the basic rate and thus pays a net amount on which tax relief is obtained. If the recipient is a registered charity the payer may obtain tax relief up to his/her higher rate whilst the charity can claim back the amount deducted.

### default
Failure by a debtor to meet the terms of a loan such as non payment of interest and capital.

### defeasance
The process of rendering a contract or deed null and void following a specified act.

### defensive securities
Securities which are considered to be more stable in price in a market where prices are falling.

### deferment period [UK]
A term used, for example, in *permanent health insurance* which refers to a period, prior to payment by the insurers to the policyholder after a claim, during which no payments

**deferred annuity**

are made. For example, a typical deferment period could be six months so if a policyholder made a claim after contracting an illness which qualified, it would be six months later that payments would commence. Sometimes an employee's company will continue paying his/her salary during this period so it would be important to ensure that the permanent health insurance links in timewise with the company's payment commitments. Also, as the deferment period increases so the premiums decrease.

**deferred annuity**
See *annuity*.

**deferred income [UK]**
Also known as income drawdown and flexible pension. See *personal pension plan*.

**deferred state pension [UK]**
When reaching retirement age, a person can elect to defer payment of his/her state pension. The result of this is to increase the value of the pension by 10% per year. There is no maximum deferment period and no further contributions are required.

**defined benefit pension plan**
A *pension* plan in which an employee's *pension* benefit is related to number of years service and *final salary* with each employer.

**defined contribution pension plan**
A *pension* plan in which benefits are dependent on contributions to and the growth of the pension fund.

**deflation**
An economic situation in which there is a general fall in the level of prices.

## demand deposit

**delinquency [USA]**
Failure to make payment on a loan obligation on the due date.

**delivery**
1. The transfer of title of a security such as stock from buyer to seller.
2. Settlement of a *futures contract* by receipt or tender of a financial instrument (for example stock) or a *commodity* or by cash settlement.

**delivery month**
See *contract month*.

**delta**
The movement of an *option* price relative to a change in the *underlying instrument* (for example shares or a commodity).

**delta shares [UK]**
A term previously given to the shares of smaller companies which were least traded on the *London Stock Exchange*, along with *alpha*, *beta* and *gamma* shares. These terms were replaced by the normal market size classification in January 1991.

**demand loan [USA]**
A loan which the lender can recall at any time. There is no specific maturity date.

**demand deposit [USA]**
A bank account balance to which the holder has instant access. The holder can withdraw funds by check or cash.

### demutualise
The conversion of a *mutual company* to a proprietary company, that is, a company with shareholders.

### denomination
The face value of currency coins and stocks and bonds.

### dental insurance
Insurance which covers dental treatment in return for regular premiums.

### Department for Work and Pensions (DWP) [UK]
Government department with a range of finance-related responsibilities including: **Jobcentre Plus**, which provides help to people looking for work and employers looking for staff; The **Pension Service**, which provides state financial support to over 11 million pensioners, as well as providing advice on planning and providing for retirement.

### deposit taking business
Money placed with financial institutions such as banks to attract *interest*.

### deposit account
An account, with a bank or financial institution, which earns interest normally proportional to and below current base rates. The notice period for withdrawal will also affect the interest rate. No cheque book is issued with a deposit account.

### Deposit Protection Scheme [UK]
A scheme formerly giving limited financial protection to persons with deposits in authorised banks which fail. Now replaced by the *Financial Services Compensation Scheme*.

### deposit insurance [USA]
Financial protection of certain bank and credit union accounts by way of insurance provided by a federal agency. Bank insurance up to specified limits is provided for funds on deposit in member banks by the *Federal Deposit Insurance Corporation*. *Credit unions* which are federally chartered are insured by the *National Credit Union Administration*.

### depreciation
The charge, as recorded in a company's accounts, which depicts the reduction in value of an asset.

### depression
A severe *recession* over a lengthened period.

### derivatives
A collective term for *futures* and *options* whose prices derive from the *underlying instrument* (for example shares or commodities etc).

### devaluation
The reduction in value of a currency with respect to another.

### devise [UK]
A *freehold* property given as a gift in a *will*.

### diluted net asset value
A method of calculating the net asset value of a company, for example an investment trust, after taking into consideration any outstanding *convertible loan stock*, *warrants* or *options* which are assumed to be exercised by the holders, so increasing the number of shares among which the assets are divided.

**Diners Club**
An international *charge card* enabling the holder to obtain goods and services without the need to pay cash. Invoices of transactions are tendered monthly which must be settled in full. There is no preset spending limit.

**direct debit**
A payment system in which the payer agrees to the payee (for example an insurance company) regularly taking funds from his/her specified bank account. This could typically be for monthly premiums for an insurance policy or for gas bills etc. If the payee needs to increase the regular amount, the customer must be informed prior to claiming the additional funds. See *standing order*.

**direct purchase [USA]**
The purchase of shares in an *open end mutual fund* directly from the fund company rather than through a broker.

**direct taxation**
Taxes which are imposed directly on the individual paying them. Examples of direct taxation are *income tax*, *capital gains tax* and *estate tax* (*inheritance tax* in the UK). See also *indirect taxation*.

**directive**
In European Union law, a directive is a piece of legislation that is binding as to the result to be achieved on all member states to which it is addressed. The exact method of achieving the result through local legislation is the responsibility of each individual state.

**disability income insurance [USA]**
Insurance which provides an income to the policyholder when he/she is unable to work due to an illness or injury. Disability

payments to insured persons, which normally commence after a set period (the *elimination period*), are usually tax free provided the premium payments are up to date.

### disclosure [USA]
The providing of all relevant information by a company, which could influence investment decisions, this in accordance with the requirements of the *Securities and Exchange Commission*.

### discount
1. The difference between the face value and the market price of a security.
2. [UK] A term used by *investment trusts* which refers to the difference between the *net asset value* per share and the share price expressed as a percentage of the net asset value per share, this being relevant whenever the share price is lower. Under these circumstances the shares are said to trade at a discount. When the share price is above the net asset value, it is said to trade at a *premium*.

### discount rate [USA]
The interest rate at which the US *Federal Reserve* lends money to member banks.

### discount yield [USA]
The yield on a security purchased at a price below its face value.

### discretionary account
An account in which an investor authorises his/her stockbroker to make purchases and sales of securities on an ongoing basis without reference or approval.

**discretionary trust**
1. A trust that enables the trustees to use their discretion in relation to the distribution of funds to beneficiaries.
2. [USA] A *mutual fund* where investments are made in a variety of differing securities depending on the decisions of the fund's management.

**disposable income**
The net amount of money available for spending from an individual's income after taxes and other deductions have been made.

**distribution**
1. The control of the sale of a large block of stock so as not to cause a fall in the price.
2. The payment of a *dividend* by a company out of its profits, or by a unit trust to unit-holders.

**distribution period**
The period following the dividend *declaration date* to the *date of record* during which a stockholder must officially own shares to be entitled to the dividend.

**diversification**
The placing of investments over a range of financial products to reduce risk.

**dividend**
The *distribution* of part of a company's earnings to shareholders. This is usually in the form of cash but can also be in the form of stock (stock dividend, or in the UK a scrip dividend).

**dividend cover**
See *cover*.

## dividend growth
The amount by which a company's yearly dividends grow compared with the previous year.

## dividend payout ratio [USA]
The dividend paid by a company expressed as a percentage of earnings. For example:
  Earnings = $1,500,000
  Dividend = $300,000.
  Dividend payout ratio = $300,000/$1,500,000 = 20%.

## dividend reinvestment
The reinvestment of dividends to purchase further shares in the company.

## dividend yield
A company's dividend per share payment divided by the current share price.

## dollar cost averaging [USA]
A plan which enables investors to accumulate shares in stock or a *mutual fund* by purchasing on a regular basis (for example monthly) with a fixed dollar amount. When the price is low, more shares will be purchased and fewer when the price is high. Also known as constant dollar plan. Known as pound cost averaging in the UK.

## domicile
The country in which a person permanently resides and in which it is the intention to remain. See also residence.

## double indemnity
A term normally associated with accident insurance. Under certain conditions, for example a road accident, a policy will pay twice the normal sum to the insured.

### double taxation
Taxation of corporate earnings and subsequently taxation of dividends.

### double taxation relief
Persons resident and domiciled in the UK are liable to *income tax* from their worldwide income payable to the *HM Revenue & Customs*. Other countries operate similar taxation rules so that there could arise a situation where an individual is subjected to double taxation. Double taxation relief can be obtained when agreements exist between countries whereby tax already paid on income in a foreign country is offset against the same tax liability in the home country or vice versa.

### Dow Jones Industrial Average
The main USA share index which monitors the movement of 30 particular industrial companies traded on the *New York Stock Exchange*.

### draft
An order in writing by one party to another party to pay a specified sum to a third party or bearer on a particular date. The party making the order or drawing the draft is known as the drawer. The party to whom the bill is addressed is the drawee (for example a bank). The party to whom the bill is payable is the payee.

### dual capital trust
See *split capital trust*.

### dual purpose fund [USA]
A closed end fund with a limited life and two main classes of shares. Holders of preferred shares receive all the income. Common shareholders receive all the fund's assets at expiry

after preferred shareholders have been paid their fixed redemption price. Similar to a *split capital investment trust* in the UK.

**durable power of attorney [USA]**
A *power of attorney* which, subject to conditions and safeguards, continues in force even after the maker of the durable power of attorney (the principal) may become mentally incapable of conducting his/her affairs.
Equivalent to lasting power of attorney in the UK.

### each way [USA]
Commission earned by a broker on both the sale and purchase of a trade.

### early retirement
For company pension schemes, an employee may retire at an early age provided it is authorised by the company. In the UK, the qualifying age is 50 (55 from 2010). However, the amount of pension payable will reduce compared with the amount payable at *normal retirement age*.

### early withdrawal penalty
A charge imposed on holders of fixed term investments in the event of withdrawal prior to maturity.

### earned income
Income such as a person's salary or wages. This is so classified since he/she has, in return, completed a job of work. This compares with such income as bank interest and company *dividends* etc which are classed as *unearned income*. Income from pensions is also classified as earned income.

### earned income credit [USA]
A tax credit for persons with at least one child living in residence for over six months and income below a certain level.

### earnest money [USA]
A deposit given to a seller by the buyer in order to demonstrate good faith and ability to complete the transaction. In the

## economics

event that the buyer fails to complete the sale, the earnest money will normally be forfeited.

**earning asset**
Any asset which produces income.

**earnings**
The annual profits of a company after deduction of tax, dividends to preferred stockholders (preference shareholders in the UK) and bondholders.

**earnings cap [UK]**
Former upper earnings limit for contributions and benefits on pension. Replaced after *A-day* by an annual contribution limit and a lifetime allowance on pension fund value.

**earnings per share (EPS)**
The *earnings* of a company divided by the number of shares of common stock (ordinary shares in the UK).

**earnings report**
See *profit and loss statement*.

**ECOFIN**
The Economic and Financial Affairs Council of the EU, made up of the Finance Ministers of all the member states (for instance the UK's Chancellor of the Exchequer).

**economics**
The study of manufacturing, distribution and consumption of products and services in an economy. This is broadly divided into macroeconomics and microeconomics. **Macroeconomics**: The study of a country's economy using such elements as unemployment, price levels, government spending, interest rates, national productivity etc and the

influence of government policy on them. **Microeconomics**: The study of economic elements at the level of the household or the company. Persons within a household are primarily concerned with employment prospects and how taxation affects their income. Companies are mainly concerned with product costs and operating expenses etc.

### effective tax rate [USA]
The ratio of tax paid in a tax year to the taxable income. For example:
   tax paid = $20,000
   taxable pay = $75,000
   effective tax rate= $20,000/$75,000= 26.7%

### electronic funds transfer system (EFTS)
An electronic payment system in which a plastic card is used to purchase goods or services. Subsequently the seller obtains payment by the electronic transfer of funds from the purchaser's card account. Equivalent to electronic funds transfer at point of sale (EFTPOS) in the UK.

### electronic money (e-money)
Defined in UK law as 'monetary value stored on an electronic device, issued on receipt of funds, and accepted as a means of payment by persons other than the issuer'. Examples are: 'electronic purse' cards that can be charged with relatively small amounts and then used in place of cash for general transactions or for specific purposes (e.g. Transport for London's Oyster card); the PayPal payment system widely used for eBay (and other) transactions.

### elimination period [USA]
The period, prior to payments to a policyholder by the insurers after a claim, during which no payments are made. Also known as waiting period. Known as deferment period in the UK.

**emergency fund**
Cash set aside in a dedicated interest account to cover unanticipated emergencies such as property repairs, medical expenses and auto repairs.

**Employee Retirement Income Security Act (ERISA) [USA]**
A federal law introduced for the protection of participants in private pension plans and health care schemes.

**employee stock ownership plan (ESOP) [USA]**
A plan devised to encourage employees to purchase stock in their company usually at a price below the market price.

**emergency tax [UK]**
A special coding used by employers when an employee's tax code is unknown. Individuals allocated this code will only receive a single person's allowance and as such may pay excessive tax (it is possible to pay insufficient tax under the emergency code). However this is corrected with a refund once the correct code becomes known and applied.

**emerging markets**
Markets which are not usually associated with traditional areas of investment. However, as their potential starts to become recognised they are seen as prospective growth areas although at higher risk.

**emoluments**
Total remuneration of an employee or director which includes salary and bonuses etc.

**endowment [USA]**
A gift such as money or property to an institution for a given purpose.

**endowment assurance [UK]**
A fixed term *life assurance* policy in which premiums pay for life cover plus a savings/investment element. The policy pays out a sum of money (the *sum assured*) on the death of the *life assured* or at a specified date (the maturity date) if the life assured survives the term. If an endowment policy is encashed in its early years any proceeds returnable to the policyholder will normally be below the value of the premiums paid up to cancellation. Variations include the low start endowment, which has reduced premiums for the first few years, and the low cost endowment, used for mortgage repayment, where the projected final value is made up of a reduced basic sum assured plus bonuses.

**endowment insurance [USA]**
A *cash value life insurance* policy with a fixed term. Premiums are applied to give life insurance cover for the face amount and at the end of the term the cash value will equate to the face amount and be payable.

**endowment mortgage [UK]**
An *interest only mortgage* which is ultimately repaid by the proceeds of an *endowment assurance* policy which is normally assigned to the lender. The policyholder pays the lender interest only, for the term of the mortgage. The sum assured, which is payable on maturity or prior death of the policyholder is used to repay the mortgage. Policies are usually *with profits* (or *low cost endowment*), *unit linked* or *unitised with profits* and sometimes this provides some additional capital for the policyholder after the lender has been repaid. However, in recent years, poor investment returns have often led to shortfalls.

**enduring power of attorney [UK]**
See *lasting power of attorney*.

### enterprise zone [UK]
A region in which companies are encouraged by the government via tax advantages to set up business. No new enterprise zones were created after 2006.

### enterprise zone trust
A property trust which invests in *enterprise zones*.

### equitable owner
The *beneficiary* designated to receive property held in trust.

### equities
Another name for the *common stock* or *ordinary shares* of companies.

### equity
The money value of an asset after deduction of debts. For example the owner of an asset valued at $8,000 who has still to repay $3,000 to a bank in conjunction with the purchase of the asset, is said to have an equity of $5,000 in the asset. The term also applies to the remaining assets in a company after all creditors have been paid.

### equity options [UK]
*Options* on the shares of companies. Equity options are traded in the UK at the *London International Financial Futures and Options Exchange* (LIFFE) and the *London Securities and Derivatives Exchange (OMLX)*.

### ERNIE [UK]
An abbreviation for Electronic Random Number Indicator Equipment which selects the prizes in the premium bonds monthly draw. See under *National Savings and Investments*, premium bonds.

**escalating annuity**
See *annuity*.

**estate**
The total value of a deceased person's assets.
For example:
Total value of property, automobile and all other
possessions = $500,000.
Allowable deductions such as mortgage, overdraft at bank, credit cards and other expenses = $ 70,000.
Total net value of estate = $430,000.

**estate agent**
An agent who acts in the arrangements of property sales and purchases in return for a commission based on the selling price and payable by the seller.

**estate duty [UK]**
A former tax on a deceased person's estate and the forerunner of *capital transfer tax* which itself has been superseded by *inheritance tax*.

**estate tax [USA]**
A tax imposed by the federal government or state on the net value of a deceased person's estate after deduction of an *exclusion*. The net proceeds, after estate tax has been paid, pass to the beneficiaries. If the sole *beneficiary* is a spouse, no tax is payable.

**estimated tax [USA]**
The estimated amount of tax owed for the forthcoming year less tax credits. A taxpayer will usually be required to pay 90% of this amount by way of *withholding* and quarterly payments or 100% (minimum) of the previous year's tax.

**euro**
The official currency of the European Union presently (2009) adopted by 16 member states (Austria, Belgium, Cyprus, Finland, France, Germany, Greece, Ireland, Italy, Luxembourg, Malta, the Netherlands, Portugal, Slovakia, Slovenia and Spain). It is also used, by agreement with the EU, by Monaco, San Marino and the Vatican – and, without formal agreement, by Andorra, Montenegro and Kosovo.

**eurobond**
A bond, issued and underwritten by international syndicates of banks and issuing houses and sold to investors (such as multinational corporations) outside the country in whose currency it is denominated. A eurobond is normally payable to the bearer and is free of tax. Note: it is not necessarily denominated in euros.

**eurocheque scheme**
A European payment scheme in which a person may purchase goods and obtain cash in the local currency of a European country outside of his/her country of residence by way of eurocheques and a guarantee card and where the EC sign is displayed. The eurocheque is debited from the person's current account after currency conversion.

**Euroclear**
A settlement system for domestic and international securities transactions, including *bonds*, *equities* and investment funds.

**eurocurrency**
A currency which is deposited in banks outside its country of origin. For example the eurodollar, eurodeutschmark and eurosterling.

## eurodollar
US dollar currency deposited in banks outside the USA.

## euromarkets
The markets in which *eurocurrencies* are traded, the largest being London.

## Euronext
A pan-European stock exchange group with a presence in Belgium, the Netherlands, France, Portugal and the UK. In 2006 merged with the New York Stock Exchange to form NYSE Euronext.

## European Economic Area (EEA)
This includes the member states of the *EU* plus three members of *EFTA*: Iceland, Liechtenstein and Norway. The EEA has an 'internal market' allowing free movement goods, services, persons and capital, in line with EU principles. The other member of EFTA, Switzerland, has a separate bilateral agreement with the EU.

## European Economic Community (EEC)
The original economic community set up in 1957 by the 6 founder members (France, West Germany, Belgium, Luxembourg, Holland and Italy) and often known as the Common Market. The expanded community now forms the *European Union*.

## European Free Trade Association (EFTA)
A grouping of countries that are unable to, or choose not to, become members of the EU. At present (2009) there are four members: Iceland, Norway, Switzerland and Liechtenstein.

## European Monetary Union (EMU)
More correctly, European Economic and Monetary Union

refers to the situation in those EU states that have adopted the euro as a common currency and submit to a common monetary policy based on interest rate levels set by the European Central Bank. A number of states (including the UK) remain outside the eurozone.

**European style option**
An *option* which may be exercised by the holder only at expiry. See also *American style option*.

**European Union (EU)**
The current (2009) member states are: Austria, Belgium, Bulgaria, Cyprus, Czech Republic, Denmark, Estonia, Finland, France, Germany, Greece, Hungary, Ireland, Italy, Latvia, Lithuania, Luxembourg, Malta, the Netherlands, Poland, Portugal, Romania, Slovakia, Slovenia, Spain, Sweden, and the UK.

**ex**
Another word for 'without'. See ex all, ex dividend, ex rights and ex scrip (UK).

**ex all**
Purchase of a security without entitlement to current *dividends*, *rights issues* or *scrip issues*. This entitlement remains with the seller of the security.

**ex dividend**
Purchase of a security without entitlement to current *dividends*. This entitlement remains with the seller of the security.

**ex gratia**
A payment made out of a sense of moral obligation. The payer however is not legally bound to do so.

**ex rights**
Purchase of a security without entitlement to current *rights issues*. This entitlement remains with the seller of the security.

**ex scrip [UK]**
Purchase of a security without entitlement to current *scrip issues*. This entitlement remains with the seller of the security.

**exceptional items**
Costs which affect a company's profit (or loss) which are associated with normal activities but are exceptional in magnitude. See *extraordinary items*.

**excess [UK]**
The specified amount a policyholder must bear before the insurers pay a *claim*. The inclusion of an excess whether compulsory or voluntary lowers the premium.

**Exchange Rate Mechanism (ERM)**
The mechanism by which members of the *EU*, prior to the adoption of the euro in 1999, operated their currency exchange rates within given upper and lower limits.

**excise duty [UK]**
A tax imposed on certain types of products including alcohol and tobacco which are produced in the UK. Customs duties apply to products imported to the UK.

**excise taxes [USA]**
Federal and state taxes on the sale or production of certain types of products such as alcohol and tobacco.

**exclusion [USA]**
1. A clause in an insurance policy which specifies items or conditions not covered.

2. An item which is excluded from taxation such as contributions to an *individual retirement account*.

**execution only account**
An account where a broker only carries out the instructions of the client and offers no advice.

**executive insurance [USA]**
An insurance policy taken out on the life of a company executive or senior employee whose death would cause significant loss to the company. In the event of such a death the proceeds would be payable to the company. Known as *key person insurance* in the UK.

**executive pension plan**
A pension plan which is tailored for directors and senior executive staff.

**executor**
A person appointed in a *will* to ensure that the wishes of the deceased are duly carried out.

**executrix**
The feminine form of *executor*.

**exemption [USA]**
An allowable expense subtracted from gross income to reduce income tax liability. An exemption can be classified as either personal or dependency and these are further subdivided into exemptions for: individual taxpayers; elderly and disabled taxpayers; dependent children and other dependants more than half of whose support is provided; total or partial blindness; a taxpayer's spouse.

### exercise
When an *option* holder takes up his/her option to buy/sell the *underlying instrument* (for example shares, commodities etc) he/she is said to exercise it.

### exercise notice
A formal notice from an *option holder* to an option *writer* that he/she wishes to buy/sell the *underlying instrument* (for example, shares, commodities etc) at the *exercise price*.

### exercise price
1. The price at which an *option* holder can buy or sell the *underlying instrument* (for example, shares, commodities etc). Also known as strike price.
2. The price which a *warrant* holder must pay for the ordinary shares of a company when the warrants are exercised.

### exit charge [UK]
Instead of making an *initial charge*, some *unit trust* companies (particularly *ISA* managers) make a charge if units are cashed in, for example, within five years. In the USA this is known as a *back end load*.

### expenses in employment
If an employee incurs expenses wholly on behalf of his/her company which are not reimbursed, such expenses can be offset against tax. Examples are accommodation, meals and fees to professional organisations.

### expiry date
1. The last day on which an *option* can be traded (*American style exercise*).
2. The only day an option can be traded (*European style option*).

**extended coverage**
Insurance which extends the term of a warranty, typically covering repairs on appliances and cars, the premium usually being a one off payment.

**extra dividend**
A dividend paid additionally to the normal dividend when profits of a company are particularly high.

**extraordinary items**
Costs which affect a company's profit (or loss) which are not associated with normal activities and which are not expected to recur. See *exceptional items*.

**extrinsic value**
See *time value*.

**face amount (face value)**
1. The value of a bond, note or other security as printed on the document. Throughout the life of a security, its price (market value) will fluctuate but at maturity the face amount is payable.
2. The value denominated on a coin, banknote or stamp etc

**fair value**
The price at which a *futures contract* should trade to be equivalent to the purchase price of the *underlying instrument*. In options trading the term is also used when referring to *intrinsic value*.

**fair market value**
The traded value of an asset agreed by seller and buyer.

**fallen angel [USA]**
A bond which was issued at a rating of AAA to BBB (investment grade) which has since fallen in rating to BB or below.
[UK] A once highly esteemed company which has undergone a down grading.

**family income benefit (family income assurance) [UK]**
A type of *term assurance* in which, following the death of the *life assured*, instalments, rather than a lump sum, are paid to the *beneficiary* for the remainder of the policy term. If the life assured lives to the end of the term, no benefit is payable.

**Fannie Mae**
See *Federal National Mortgage Association*.

**fat cat**
An individual able to create additional wealth from the investment of existing substantial assets. In the UK the term also refers to executives who have earned high salaries and bonuses on the performance of privatised companies and other organisations etc.

**federal agency security [USA]**
A debt instrument with a high level of safety issued by a federal agency.

**Federal Deposit Insurance Corporation (FDIC) [USA]**
The federal agency that acts as guarantor for funds deposited in member banks, up to a maximum of $100,000 (£250,000 until 1 January 2010).

**federal gift tax [USA]**
A federal tax levied on gifted property, money or securities. The tax is payable by the donor and based on *fair market value* of the gift. A parent or parents making gifts to children are allowed to make transfers up to a specified amount without paying tax.

**Federal Insurance Contributions Act (FICA) [USA]**
The federal law which directs employers to withhold a proportion of employees' salaries for payment to the government in order to provide future pension and other social security benefits.

**Federal National Mortgage Association (FNMA) [USA]**
A government backed corporation which purchases mortgages from lenders and resells them to investors. It is financed by

### Federal Reserve System

the issue of debt securities. Equity shares, known as Fannie Maes, are traded on the *New York Stock Exchange*.

### Federal Reserve System [USA]
The American central banking system which comprises 12 regional Federal Reserve Banks, their branches and all national and state banks within the system. The Federal Reserve sets monetary policy in the USA and regulates the banking system.

### Fedwire [USA]
A computerized high speed communication system linking the banks within the *Federal Reserve System*. The network enables transfers to be conducted at high speed for inter-bank dealings and customer transfers.

### fiduciary
A person entrusted to manage the assets and interests of another. For example, an *executor* in a will would be so described.

### final dividend
The end of year dividend. In the UK, companies normally pay dividends twice per year, an interim and a final dividend, the latter normally being the larger of the two and being declared at the *annual general meeting*. See *dividend*.

### final salary [UK]
The basis of determining a person's pension entitlement in a *final salary scheme* and which normally refers to an *occupational pension*. Final salary is defined as either:
1. the total *emoluments* in a year, in any of the five years immediately preceding retirement or
2. the average of total emoluments for periods of three consecutive years or more ending within ten years

of retirement. (Directors who own 20% or more of a company's share capital must define their final salary according to 2.above).

## final salary scheme (defined benefit scheme)
A *pension* scheme in which an employee's pension is based on his/her number of years service and *final salary* with each employer. In this type of scheme employees are typically provided with 1/60 of final salary for each year of service up to a maximum of 40/60 that is, two thirds of final salary. At retirement a tax free lump sum may be taken at the expense of a reduced pension.

## finance house
A company whose main purpose is the financing of hire purchase transactions.

## financial adviser
A professional person qualified to give advice to clients regarding investments such as life insurance, pensions, mutual funds/unit trusts and taxation etc. A financial adviser may charge a fee and/or receive a commission on a product recommended. In the UK a financial adviser is either independent that is, *an independent financial adviser (IFA)*, or a *company representative* of one or a limited range of companies (tied agent). An independent financial adviser is free to recommend products from a number of companies and his/her selection will be based on which company and product would best suit the needs of the client. A company representative is authorised to recommend only the products of the company/companies he/she represents.

## financial futures
*Futures contracts* where the *underlying instruments* are financial such as shares, interest rates, currencies and indexes etc.

## Financial Industry Regulatory Authority [USA]
Regulatory body for the US securities industry formed in 2007 by the merger of *NASD* and the regulation committee of the *New York Stock Exchange*.

### financial institution
An institution which accepts funds from the public and reinvests in bank deposits, bonds and stocks etc. These include banks and insurance companies. In the UK a *building society* would be included.

### financial intermediary
An institution such as a bank, that accepts funds from various sources and redistributes such funds to other parties whilst making its profit. Basically an intermediary is a go between for those who possess surplus money wishing to earn interest and those who require short or long term loans who will pay a higher rate of interest than those depositing.

### Financial Ombudsman Service [UK]
This organisation provides an independent facility for the resolution of complaints and disputes between financial services firms and their clients, when a firm's internal complaints procedure has been exhausted without the customer obtaining satisfaction.

### financial pager
A pocket sized pager with datascreen which can display a variety of financial information including equities, bonds, futures and market news etc plus facilities for alert for limit breaches. The type of information transmitted is dependent on the service provider.

### financial planner
A professional person qualified to give clients a *financial planning* service.

### financial planning
A service provided by a financial planner. This is a long term service provided for clients which considers all their financial affairs and which develops a plan for their financial objectives to be achieved. The plan is regularly reviewed to ensure goals remain on target with modifications being made as necessary.

### Financial Services Act 1986 [UK]
A Government Act introduced primarily to provide increased protection for investors and to regulate investment business conducted in the UK.

### Financial Services and Markets Act 2000 [UK]
Expanding on and superseding the Financial Services Act 1986, this Act established the basis for supervision of virtually the whole of the UK financial services industry by the Financial Services Authority.

### Financial Services Authority (FSA) [UK]
The FSA came into being in 1997 (replacing the Securities and Investments Board (SIB)), and carries all regulatory responsibilities for the UK financial services industry. The overall broad objectives are the protection of consumers of financial services, the promotion of clean and orderly markets and the maintenance of confidence in the financial services system. It is a criminal offence to conduct investment business without authorisation and the FSA is empowered to prosecute those who break this rule. The FSA maintains a Register, which is a public record of financial services firms, individuals and other bodies under its regulatory jurisdiction. The FSA Register is available online.

### Financial Services Compensation Scheme [UK]
Provides compensation for clients who have lost money as a result of the insolvency of a firm authorised by the *FSA*.

Separate sub-schemes apply to the insolvency of: insurance companies; investment firms; banks and building societies; mortgage advisers and arrangers.

### financial statement
A statement which lists a balance sheet (depicting assets, liabilities and capital), income statement, cash flow statement and net worth.

### Financial Times Indices [UK]
A wide range of indices including shares, stocks and fixed interest securities published by the Financial Times. The indices serve as indicators of trends of prices on the *London Stock Exchange* and foreign exchanges. The best known is the FT-SE 100 Index (Footsie).

### first mortgage
A mortgage which carries priority over any subsequent *second mortgage*. In the event of default, the lender (mortgagee) providing the first mortgage will receive precedence.

### fiscal policy
The use of spending and taxation by the government in order to achieve its economic objectives. See *monetary policy*.

### fiscal year
The tax year set by the government. It commences on: 1 October in the USA, 6 April in the UK; 1 July in Australia.

### fixed annuity [USA]
An *annuity* which guarantees payments to an annuitant which are fixed for life or a specific period. Similar to a level annuity in the UK.

## fixed assets
Assets of a company such as buildings and machinery which are regularly used over a long period of time for the purpose of generating profits.

## fixed income securities
Securities such as government, municipal and corporate bonds which pay a fixed rate of interest until maturity. Also *preferred stock* where fixed payments are referred to as dividends.

## fixed rate mortgage
A type of *mortgage* where interest repayments to the lender are fixed until maturity or for a specified term.

## flat yield
The return (interest) on a *fixed interest security* expressed as a percentage of its current market price. See also *bond yield*.

## flexible pension [UK]
Also known as deferred income, income drawdown or unsecured pension. See *personal pension plan*.

## flotation
The establishment of a public company by an *offer for sale* of shares to the public or by a *placing*. This enables the company to raise capital for its future growth. Known as an *initial public offering (IPO)* in the USA.

## footsie
The Financial Times 100 Share Index (FTSE 100 Index).

## foreclosure
The procedure by which a homeowner forfeits his/her property to the lender (mortgagee) following default. This could be failure to pay interest on the loan. A foreclosure order is given by a court.

### force majeure
Unforeseeable events, beyond the control of participants in a contract, which may excuse either side from fulfilling its liabilities.

### foreign exchange
Currencies issued by foreign countries.

### forward dealing
The buying or selling of *underlying instruments* such as *commodities*, securities and currencies etc for delivery at a specified future date and a fixed price.

### forward pricing
1. The setting of the price (which then remains fixed) for *forward dealing*. This occurs at the time the contract is established.
2. The selling of unit trusts at a price to be determined at the end of the dealing period.

### fourth market [USA]
The market of securities trading without the participation of brokers, thus obviating commission costs. The market, which is computer based, mainly comprises large institutional investors such as mutual funds and insurance companies.

### franchise
A licence, granted by one company (franchisor) to another company or person (franchisee/licence holder), entitling the licence holder to produce or market a product in a specific area. The licence is usually reviewed periodically, typically every 6 months or annually.

### franchisee
See *franchise*.

## franchisor
See *franchise*.

## franked income [UK]
Dividends, paid by UK companies to other companies (for example, investment trusts), with a tax credit reflecting the fact that the company which has paid the dividend has done so out of post tax profits. Therefore the 'franked income' will be free of further tax to the receiving company.

## free standing additional voluntary contributions (FSAVC) [UK]
An employee's pension scheme which is additional to but independent from his/her *occupational pension scheme*. Since *A-Day*, employees have been able to use personal pensions to top up their occupational pensions, so the market for FSAVCs has reduced.

## freehold [UK]
The permanent ownership of land or buildings which can be legally passed on to heirs, it is the most usual form of ownership for houses. Also known as property that is held in 'fee simple'.

## friendly society [UK]
A *mutual organisation* whose funds, after the deduction of running costs, are owned by its policyholders. The main purpose of a friendly society is to provide life assurance and to assist members during sickness and unemployment. They were first formed around the sixteenth century in order to provide protection for the families of working individuals in the event of their death or illness. As a result of this of this history they still enjoy favourable tax treatment of their investment funds, within specified limits. Formerly regulated by the Friendly Societies Commission, they are now regulated by the *Financial Services Authority (FSA)*.

### fringe benefits
Benefits to employees additional to salary. Typical examples would be company cars, expense accounts and private medical insurance which in the USA are not normally taxable. However they would be liable for tax in the UK.

### front end load
A charge imposed by a management company on a *mutual fund* or *unit trust* to cover administration costs and commission at the time of purchase.

### FTSE All Share Index
The Financial Times' index of the share prices of over 98% of the UK market capitalisation from all sectors, it is a reflection of the general trend of the market. The performance of funds under management are often compared with this index. See below examples of other Financial Times' Indices.

### FTSE 350 Index
A combined index of the *FTSE 100* and the *FTSE 250*.

### FTSE 100 Index (Footsie)
An index of the share prices of the 100 largest companies (by *market capitalisation*) in the UK which is constantly updated. The index was started in 1984 with a base of 1,000.

### FTSE 250 Index
An index of the share prices of the 250 largest companies (by *market capitalisation*) immediately following the largest 100 (FT-SE 100).

### FT Eurotop 100
An index of the share prices of the 100 largest European blue chip companies (by *market capitalisation*).

**full disclosure**
The obligation to disclose all factual information relevant to a contract.

**full endowment mortgage [UK]**
A mortgage supported by a with-profit endowment with a basic sum assured equal to the loan amount.

**full faith and credit [USA]**
Effectively a guarantee of payment of interest and repayment of principal of a bond issued by a government authority.

**full structural**
An extensive property survey.

**fully invested**
When all money in a portfolio is invested in securities as opposed to retaining some cash, it is said to be fully invested.

**fully paid policy**
A *life insurance* policy which remains in force where the *insured* has paid premiums over part of the term of the policy but is unable to make further payments. In these circumstances the cash or surrender value is used to purchase a single premium policy which pays a reduced amount either on the death of the insured or on maturity if a term is specified other than life.

**fund**
A pool of money normally set apart for a purpose, for example, a pension fund to provide pensions.

**fund switching**
The movement of assets in one *mutual fund* or *unit trust* to another within a range of funds with differing objectives, all managed by the same investment company

**fund value**
The monetary value of a *fund*.

**fundamental analysis**
The analysis of a company's financial statement so as to forecast future growth prospects and assess whether the current share price is properly valued.

**further advance**
The raising of capital by a mortgagor (borrower) from his/her existing mortgagee (lender). This could occur when for example both the value of the property and the mortgagor's salary has increased over the years. Under these circumstances the existing lender may consider the advancing of further capital to the mortgagor provided he/she can afford the higher repayments. The interest rate will not necessarily be the same as the existing rate but usually similar.

**futures**
See *futures contract*.

**futures contract**
A legal agreement to make or take delivery of a specified instrument (for example, a commodity such as coffee or a financial instrument such as shares) at a fixed future date at a price determined at the time of dealing.

## gain
The difference between the selling price and purchase price of a *security*. See capital gains tax.

## gamma shares [UK]
A term previously given to the shares of smaller companies traded far less frequently on the *London Stock Exchange* than alpha and beta shares. These terms were replaced by the *normal market size* classification in January 1991.

## garnishee
The recipient (typically a bank) to whom a *garnishee order* has been delivered.

## garnishee order [UK]
A court order instructing a garnishee (a bank) that funds held on behalf of a debtor (the judgement debtor) should not be released until directed by the court. The order may also instruct the bank to pay a given sum to the judgement creditor (the person to whom a debt is owed by the judgement debtor) from these funds.

## garnishment [USA]
A court order instructing an employer to withhold all or part of an employee's salary and to submit this amount (and subsequent amounts if relevant) to the court for settlement of a debt or other legal obligation to another party.

*gearing*

**gearing [UK]**
1. The capital structure of a company which is the ratio of its debt (loan capital such as debentures etc) to its equity capital (ordinary share capital plus retained profits). The American term for gearing is *leverage*. Where a company is financed largely by loan capital rather than by equity capital, it is said to be highly geared.
2. A term which refers to borrowings by an *investment trust* which boost the return on capital and income via additional investment. When the trust is performing well shareholders enjoy an enhanced or geared profit. However if the trust performs poorly then the loss is similarly exaggerated.
3. A term used in *warrants* which refers to the ratio between a company's share price and its warrant price.

**General Agreement on Tariffs and Trade (GATT)**
A trade agreement between a large number of countries, dating back to 1948, which was set up to improve trading worldwide and to work towards the reduction of tariff barriers. Overtaken in 1995 by the establishment of the *World Trade Organisation*, when most GATT signatories became members of WTO.

**general insurance [UK]**
The term is used for all forms of insurance that are not long-term insurance. In other words it includes household, motor, public liability etc, but not life assurance. See *insurance*.

**general lien**
The legal right for a *creditor* to seize the assets of a *debtor* to satisfy an outstanding debt.

**general obligation bond [USA]**
A municipal bond whose interest and principal payments are supported by the *full faith and credit* of the issuing authority.

## gilt edged securities

**genetic testing**
A form of medical analysis that can identify the genes that may cause certain types of illness. Debate still rages as to whether its use is appropriate for underwriting life assurance. In the UK a voluntary ban on its use in relation to life cover up to £500,000 is in force until 2011.

**gift**
A transfer of an asset such as property or money etc from one person to another where no payment of any kind is given by the receiving person to the donor.
[UK] Transfers of this kind may be subject to inheritance tax if the value is above a certain amount and to capital gains tax in certain circumstances.

**gift tax [USA]**
A tax imposed by the federal government or state on the donor of a gift when the transfer of money or property passes from one individual to another. A parent or parents making gifts to children are allowed to make transfers up to a specified amount without paying tax. In the UK there is currently no gift tax in operation although there is a potential liability for *inheritance tax* when gifts are made. See potentially exempt transfer (PET).

**gilt edged securities [USA]**
Bonds of companies with a high reputation for dependency for the payment of bond interest.
[UK] (gilts) Fixed interest stocks issued by the British Government and called gilts because of the gilt edged surround on original certificates. These stocks (or securities) are traded on the *London Stock Exchange* and their prices influenced by items such as interest rates and other market conditions. Gilt prices are normally quoted per £100 of nominal value and if they are (what are known as)

*redeemable*, the £100 is repaid to whoever happens to be the owner at the *redemption date*. Redeemable gilts are classified as longs (redeemable after fifteen years or more), mediums (redeemable between five and fifteen years) and shorts (redeemable within five years). Income from gilts is liable for tax but all capital gains are tax free. In the USA the equivalent government debt instruments are *Treasury securities*.

**Gilt Edged Market Makers (GEMMs)**
*Market makers* dealing in gilts.

**gilts**
See *gilt edged securities* [UK].

**Ginnie Mae**
See *Government National Mortgage Association (GNMA)*.

**Girobank [UK]**
Girobank was established in 1968 and known then as the National Girobank. It was set up by the Post Office and provided a public banking facility for people without bank accounts. Now part of Alliance and Leicester Commercial Bank.

**global fund [USA]**
A mutual fund which invests in securities in countries around the world such as Europe and Asia as well as the USA.

**going long**
See *long position*.

**going short**
See *short position*.

**gold card**
A plastic payment card which normally allows the holder higher spending limits over the standard card. Also loan facilities are sometimes available. Persons holding such a card are often required to be earning a minimum salary level. Gold cards are usually either ***charge cards*** or ***credit cards***.

**good till cancelled order**
An order to a broker to buy or sell a security at a specified price which remains valid until cancelled by the client or by execution.

**government securities**
See ***gilt edged securities***.

**Government National Mortgage Association (GNMA) [USA]**
A government owned corporation which guarantees payment of interest and principal of mortgage backed ***pass through securities***. The corporation is nicknamed Ginnie Mae.

**grace period**
The period, normally 30 days during which an insurance policy remains in force even though the premium has not been paid.

**graduated payment mortgage (GPM) [USA]**
A mortgage scheme in which monthly payments commence at a lower level and increase over a period of a few years to a higher level which is subsequently maintained.

**Graduated Pension [UK]**
A former supplementary state pension (supplementary to the basic state pension), a predecessor of SERPS and the current S2P.

**granny bonds [UK]**
Once a popular name for NS&I index-linked savings certificates, because they were originally introduced for people who were over retirement age.

**grantee [UK]**
A term, used by some assurance companies, as an alternative to *assured*.

**grant of probate**
See *probate*.

**gray knight [USA] grey knight [UK]**
A company (or person), making an unwanted counter bid for another company, whose intentions are unclear. See *black knight* and *white knight*.

**gross**
Before any deductions.

**gross domestic product (GDP)**
The value of all goods and services created within an economy over a specified time which is usually one year.

**gross income [USA]**
The total income of a person (salary, dividend and interest income, capital gains etc) before *exclusions* and *deductions*.
[UK] The total income of a person prior to the subtraction of *tax allowances*. This for example could be a person's salary plus bonuses plus benefits in kind (company car and medical insurance) plus income from shares etc. See *net income*.

## gross interest
1. Interest earned by deposits at banks and financial institutions, also *gilts* etc before deduction of tax.
2. Interest charged on bank loans etc before any tax relief is taken into account.

## gross margin
The difference between the selling price of an item and the purchase or manufacturing cost, expressed as a percentage of the selling price. For example a company's manufacturing cost of an item is $6 and the selling price is $10. Gross margin = [($10 -$6)/£10] x 100 = 40%.

## gross national product (GNP)
The addition of *gross domestic product* and various forms of income from abroad.

## gross profit
1. The difference between the selling price of an item and the purchase or manufacturing cost.
2. A company's total turnover of products sold less costs to purchase or manufacture. See *net profit*.

## gross rate
1. The interest rate earned by deposits at banks and financial institutions before deduction of tax, for example, 5% gross rate.
2. The interest rate charged on bank loans, and mortgage interest etc before any tax relief is taken into account.

## gross redemption yield
See *redemption yield*.

## gross yield
The *yield* on a *security* before the deduction of tax.

## grossing up
The adjusting of a net return on an investment to the gross equivalent, that is adding back the tax deducted to obtain the gross return.

## ground rent [UK]
Rent payable by the owner of a *leasehold property* to the *freehold* owner.

## group insurance
Insurance provided for company employees by employers, for instance health insurance, disability insurance and term life insurance. It would be considerably more expensive for a single employee to obtain such insurance.

## Group of Seven (G7)
The seven foremost industrial countries outside what was the communist bloc. They are USA, Germany, Japan, United Kingdom, France, Canada and Italy. The main objectives are the discussions of economic and political issues of common interest to the group.

## Group of Twenty (G20)
Brings together the Finance Ministers and Central Bank governors of 20 important industrialised and developing economies. Members are Argentina, Australia, Brazil, Canada, China, France, Germany, India, Indonesia, Italy, Japan, Mexico, Russia, Saudi Arabia, South Africa, South Korea, Turkey, the UK and the USA, plus the EU. The World Bank and the IMF are also represented at meetings.

## growth
An asset which increases in value.

## growth and income fund
A *mutual fund* or *unit trust* which aims to provide investors with continuing dividend payments plus capital gains.

## growth fund
A *mutual fund* or *unit trust* which aims to provide investors with capital growth

## growth bond
A bond which gives capital growth at maturity.

## growth stocks
Stocks (shares) whose share values have grown at an above average rate over a number of years and which are expected to continue to grow at a high rate.

## guarantee
1. A commitment made by a person to be answerable for the debts or liabilities of another.
2. [UK] A document, supplied by a manufacturer, indicating that in the event of product failure it will be repaired or replaced. This usually involves a specified time period. In the USA this is known as a warranty.

## guaranteed death benefit [UK]
The minimum sum payable by a life policy on the death of the *life assured*.

## guaranteed growth bond
A bond in which a single premium secures a guaranteed amount at its maturity date.

## guaranteed income bond
A bond in which a single premium secures a guaranteed regular income until maturity at which time the original premium is returned.

**guaranteed minimum pension [UK]**
The minimum pension payable by a pension scheme in order that members may contract out of the additional state pension (e.g. *SERPS*). Applied only to periods of pension scheme membership prior to April 1997.

**guaranteed minimum period**
The period during which an *annuity* is paid irrespective of whether the *annuitant* dies during that period. If the annuitant lives beyond this period, payments continue until death. An annuity with such a guarantee could benefit people, with dependants, who require the income to continue after their death. This means that the sum of money paid for the annuity would not be wasted in the event of early death.

**guaranteed renewable policy**
An insurance policy which is guaranteed renewable provided premiums are paid. The policy conditions remain unchanged although the insurers may review premium rates.

**guaranteed sum assured [UK]**
A term used by some life companies which refers to the minimum sum payable by a life policy either on the death of the *life assured* or on maturity.

**guarantor**
A person who commits to guarantee the debts of another. For example if an individual fails to meet his/her obligations on say hire purchase repayments, the guarantor will be obliged to make those repayments.

### Hang Seng Index
The main indicator of stock market performance in Hong Kong based on 42 companies. The index is arithmetically calculated and weighted by *market capitalisation*.

### hard currency
A currency which is generally accepted throughout the world and which is unlikely to devalue. Examples are the euro, US dollar and Swiss franc.

### hard dollars [USA]
Payment to a broker (excluding the earning of any commissions) by a customer for services provided. This payment could be for advice or for providing a financial plan.

### health insurance [USA]
Generic term for insurance covering costs incurred due to illness, injury and disability.

### heavy market [USA]
A market in which there are more sellers than buyers resulting in falling prices.

### hedge fund
An investment fund, generally open to a limited range of investors, often wealthy individuals who are prepared to take risks and back the judgement of a particular fund manager. As implied by the name, they often offset possible losses by hedging, particularly by *short selling*.

### hedge ratio
The number of *futures* or *options* contracts required to *hedge*/counteract the exposure in the **underlying instrument** (for example shares, commodities etc).

### hedging (hedge)
A strategy employed in a *futures* market to reduce risk. This is achieved by establishing a position which is broadly opposite to that held in the **underlying instrument** (for example shares, commodities etc).

### Her Majesty's Revenue & Customs [UK]
The government department which collects income tax, customs and excise duties and *VAT*. Formed by a merger of the Inland Revenue and HM Customs and Excise.

### hidden values [USA]
Assets owned by a company but undervalued on the balance sheet and accordingly not exhibited in the stock price. Similar to hidden reserve in the UK.

### high current income fund [USA]
A mutual fund which seeks to pay a high dividend to its shareholders. This may be by way of *junk bonds* which pay higher levels of income but with the attendant higher risk.

### high equity
A *mortgage* which is low in comparison to the amount deposited in cash by the purchaser.

### high grade security [USA]
A bond, issued by a highly regarded company or municipal authority with a rating of AAA or AA.

### high-tech stocks
The stocks of companies participating in high technology fields such as computers, semiconductors and electronics.

### higher rate adjustment [UK]
An *income tax* coding which is relevant to persons who pay tax at the higher rate. For interest received from banks or *dividends* from shares etc, the higher rate adjustment enables the Inland Revenue to collect the additional tax due over and above the *basic rate*. The additional tax can, if required, be paid separately.

### higher rate tax [UK]
The highest rate of *income tax* in the UK which is immediately above the *basic rate*.

### hire purchase
A transaction in which the purchaser of goods pays an initial deposit and takes possession. Subsequent instalments are made over a specified time after which ownership passes to the purchaser.

### historical volatility
See *volatility*.

### holder
1. A person in possession of a *negotiable instrument* such as a *bill of exchange* or *promissory note*. That person may be the payee or the endorsee.
2. A person who has made an *opening purchase* of an *option* and thus has acquired the rights to them.

### holder of record [USA]
The owner of securities whose name is registered by the issuing company or its *transfer agent* as from a particular date.

### holding company
A company which holds the majority of shares in its subsidiaries. Also known as the parent company.

### holding period [USA]
The length of time an individual retains hold of an investment. If an investment is held for more than one year the capital gain liability is reduced.

### holiday insurance [UK]
A policy which covers the *insured* and usually his/her family for the duration of their holiday. Items covered normally include travel delays, unavoidable cancellation, baggage loss and damage, loss of personal items including cash and credit cards, personal accident and medical expenses abroad.

### home banking
A facility provided by banks enabling customers to conduct banking transactions by telephone or on the internet. This system allows instant access to bank balances and the provision for transferring funds.

### home income plan [UK]
Also known as a lifetime mortgage, this plan enables older people to release some of the equity in their house (often to provide additional income) whilst remaining in the property. The property is mortgaged and the interest is either paid out the income derived from investing the funds received, or – more commonly – is rolled up and paid out of the sale proceeds of the house on the death of the customer (or second death of a couple).

### home reversion plan [UK]
Similar to a *home income plan* except that instead of being mortgaged, the property or a share in it is sold to the finance

company in exchange for funds. The customer is allowed to remain in the property for the duration of their lifetime.

**homeowners equity account [USA]**
A credit line offered by banks and mortgage lenders which grants the homeowner the opportunity of borrowing against the built up equity in the property.

**homeowners insurance [USA]**
A form of property insurance which provides cover against such items as damage to the building, personal property, theft, personal liability etc.

**hospital income policy [USA] hospital cash plan [UK]**
An insurance policy which pays a specified amount to the insured in the event that he/she goes to hospital. This is usually to provide for lost income.

**hostile takeover**
A takeover bid by one company for another, the latter being opposed to such a bid.

**house call [USA]**
The notification to a client by a brokerage house that more funds are required to bring a *margin account* balance up to the required level.

**household insurance [UK]**
Insurance covering the structure or contents of a house. This type of insurance now tends to include the option of cover for additional items such as legal expenses. Also some companies now offer no claims bonuses similar to those given by motor insurance companies. See buildings insurance and contents insurance.

## identified shares [USA]
The shares of stock or a *mutual fund* carrying a record of purchase price and date of purchase. For example if shares are being accumulated through a *constant dollar plan* there will be an ongoing record of all share purchase prices and purchase dates which enables the *cost basis* to be established. When shares are sold the owner can identify those which were purchased at higher prices in order to keep capital gains tax to a minimum.

## identity theft
The fraudulent use of another person's personal and financial information in order to take money from their accounts or to withdraw money from bogus accounts established using their details.

## IFA Promotion [UK]
An organisation established in 1989 to improve the image of *Independent Financial Advisers (IFAs)* and their work and to encourage consumers to seek independent financial advice. It aims to help members of the public to find local IFAs to consult.

## immediate annuity
See *annuity*.

## in house
A term used in banking which refers to settlement of payments between accounts both held at the same branch.

### in the money
1. A call option with an *exercise price* below, or a *put option* with an exercise price above the *underlying instrument* (for example shares, commodities). They are said to have *intrinsic value*.
2. Warrants with an exercise price below the market price.

### incapacity benefit [UK]
A state benefit payable to people who cannot work due to sickness or disability, and are unable to claim *statutory sick pay* (e.g. the self-employed).

### incentive stock option [USA]
A stock option, available only to employees of the issuing firm, which is free of federal income tax when granted and when exercised. The option must be exercised within ten years, and any gain made may be subject to capital gains tax.

### income
1. Salary, wages or fees received in return for work carried out.
2. Money received from investments, for example bank interest and share dividends.

### income bond
A bond which provides income over its life and at maturity the original investment is returned. See *guaranteed income bond*.

### income dividend [USA]
A distribution of interest or dividends to the shareholders of a *mutual fund*.

### income drawdown [UK]
Also known as deferred income and flexible pension. See *personal pension plan*.

### income fund [USA]
A *mutual fund* whose aim is to provide shareholders with *current income*.

### income from property [UK]
Income received from property letting is subject to income tax. The amount taxable is the amount receivable in the tax year. If an owner occupier or tenant rents out a room he/she may receive up to a certain annual income without incurring a tax liability.

### income limit for age related allowances [UK]
Persons aged 65 to 74 are entitled to an additional personal tax allowance provided total earnings do not exceed a given amount. This allowance is further increased for persons aged 75 and over. In cases where total earnings exceed this figure, these allowances are reduced by £1 for every £2 of income earned above this amount, down to a minimum of the under-65 personal allowance.

### income shares
1. Shares purchased in anticipation of an above average income being produced. Also referred to as high *yield* shares.
2. Those shares in a *dual purpose fund* (*split capital investment trust* in the UK) which receive most or all of the trust's income. The other class of shares (capital shares) receive the fund's capital.

### income stock [USA]
A reputable stock with a record of consistently high dividend payments to shareholders.

### income tax [USA]
The taxation of income by the federal government, state and local governments. *Taxable income*, on which tax

liability is computed, is assessed by subtracting deductions and exemptions from gross income. There is a range of tax brackets and as taxable income increases from one bracket to another the tax rate increases.

[UK] The *direct taxation* of a person's earned income (for example salary/wages) and unearned income (for example building society interest and share dividends). The tax is levied on *gross income* less allowances and reliefs, this being known as taxable income.

**income tax allowances**
See *tax allowances*.

**income tax schedules**
See *Taxation Schedules*.

**increasing life annuity**
Another expression for *escalating annuity*. See *annuity*.

**increasing term assurance**
See *term assurance*.

**indemnity**
An agreement in which one person is answerable for restoring the losses of another.

**indemnity commission**
Where a life company pays upfront commission to an agent, the company does so on the proviso it will be entitled to take back (*clawback*)some or all of such commission if the relevant policy is cancelled within a given period.

**indemnity insurance**
A policy which covers the *insured* against the loss of an asset or incurring a liability by reimbursement of money etc. The

purpose of such insurance is to place the insured in exactly the same financial state after a loss as he/she was in before such loss occurred.

### indenture [USA]
A written agreement (also called a deed of trust) between a bond issuer and a purchaser which details: description of bond; amount of the issue; property pledged if not a debenture; covenants; working capital and current ratio; redemption rights or privileges. A trustee also acts on behalf of all bondholders.
**[UK]** A written agreement between two persons. This term is used between a master and an apprentice.

### independent financial adviser (IFA)
See *financial adviser*.

### index
A number which represents a set of data and which is measured on an ongoing basis with a view to tracking changes from a given base. For example, the *consumer price index* gives a measure of the change in the cost of living. The *Standard and Poor's Composite Index (S&P 500)* measures the share prices of 500 US companies and reflects the general trend of the US stock market. The FTSE 100 Index is a measure of the combined share prices of the 100 largest companies in the UK.

### index fund
A fund which invests to perform in line with a stock exchange index such as the Standard and Poor's 500 Index and the FTSE 100 Index in the UK. Over the long term it is argued that very few fund managers outperform the index against which their funds are compared. Also because costs are kept to a minimum (no fees for active fund management), an

investment in an index fund will purchase more shares or units than in a managed fund. Sometimes known as a tracker fund.

**index linked**
The coupling of such items as salaries and pensions etc to the *retail price index* in order to take account of *inflation*.

**index linked family income assurance [UK]**
*Family income assurance* in which the *assured* may, if he or she chooses, increase premiums in line with the *retail price index* and hence increase the *sum assured*.

**index linked term assurance [UK]**
*Term assurance* in which premiums are increased in line with the *retail price index* and hence the *sum assured* is increased.

**index options**
Call or put options on an index such as the Standard and Poor's 500 Index or the FTSE 100 Index. Such options are exercisable into cash rather than the underlying shares as is the case with *equity options*. In the USA, index options are traded on a number of exchanges including the New York and Chicago Board Options Exchanges. In the UK, index options are traded on the *London International Financial Futures and Options Exchange. (LIFFE)*

**indexation**
The factor by which wages and pensions etc are multiplied in order to be linked to an index. This factor is intended to account for *inflation*. In the USA indexing wages to the *consumer price index (CPI)* may apply. In the UK indexation of items such as wages and pensions to the *retail price index* may be relevant. See *indexation allowance*.

### indexation allowance [UK]
An allowance formerly given against capital gains tax (CGT) which took into account increases in the values of assets (for example shares) due to *inflation*.
This allowance was frozen as at April 1998, and then withdrawn altogether in 2008. See *capital gains tax*.

### indirect taxation
Taxation which is paid to the government in an indirect way, for example in the UK, *value added tax (VAT)* charged on goods and services. VAT is the main indirect tax in the UK and is ultimately paid by the consumer. However the consumer may be said to have the choice as to whether or not goods or services are purchased whereas *direct taxation* is paid automatically when, for example, a person's income, capital gains or *estate* values exceed a certain level.

### individual retirement account (IRA) [USA]
A *tax deferred* retirement savings account which may be set up by persons in employment. Annual contributions are limited (2009 figures) to earned income or $5,000, whichever is less, for individuals under age 50 ($6,000 at 50 or over). IRA contributions are generally tax deductible and savings grow tax free over the term of the plan, but when pension benefits are taken, they will be liable to tax.

### individual savings account (ISA) [UK]
A tax favoured savings account introduced in 1999 to replace *PEP*s and *TESSA*s. They are free from tax on income and capital gains, except that fund managers of equity ISAs cannot reclaim the 10% tax credit deducted from UK share dividends. They are available to persons aged 18 or over (16 or over for cash ISAs). There are two types: cash ISAs based on bank and building society deposit accounts, and equity

## *initial margin*

ISAs, which can contain shares, corporate bonds, gilt-edged stocks, unit trusts, OEICs and investment trusts. The overall annual subscription limit for ISAs (in 2009/10) is £7,200, of which up to £3,600 p.a. can be in a cash ISA component.

### industrial life assurance [UK]
An *assurance* policy on the life of an individual where weekly or monthly premiums are regularly paid to the assurance company by way of their agent who collects directly from the policyholder's home. This method of collection originated in industrial areas as a means of saving for a future lump sum or protection against industrial accidents etc. This type of assurance is now virtually extinct.

### inflation
The increasing of wages and prices in an economy over a period of time, usually annualised for comparative purposes.

### inheritance tax [UK]
A tax charged on the assets of a deceased person's *estate* above a tax free allowance known as the nil-rate band. There is an additional charge on gifts over £3,000 in any year given within the 7 years preceding death which is made on a diminishing scale. See *potentially exempt transfer (PET)*. The rate of inheritance tax charged on death is 40%.

### initial charge
A charge imposed by a management company on a *unit trust* to cover administration costs (also known as front end load).

### initial margin [USA]
Payment required to be made by an investor to a broker to open a *margin account*. Once initial margin is deposited

## initial public offering

the investor may deal on credit from the broker. The credit extended is directly related to the margin deposited which itself is dependent on the purchase price of a securities transaction.

[UK] The returnable, initial outlay of money required from a *futures* or *options* trader as security against default.

### initial public offering (IPO) [USA]
The first offering of a corporation's stock to the public. Known as a flotation in the UK.

### Inland Revenue [UK]
The government department formerly responsible to the Treasury for the collection of direct taxes which include *income tax, capital gains tax* and *inheritance tax* etc. Now merged with the former HM Customs and Excise as ***HM Revenue and Customs***.

### input tax [UK]
When a company or trader, registered for *value added tax (VAT)*, purchases goods or services from another supplier, VAT is additionally payable and is normally 17.5% (15% during 2009) of the purchase cost. This is known as input tax. Similarly, sales from the company or trader attract VAT at the same rate. This is known *as output tax*.

The difference between output tax and input tax is payable to HM Revenue & Customse. In the event of input tax being greater than output tax, such as when starting up a new business, this difference is reclaimable from HM Revenue & Customs.

### insider dealing
The use of confidential company information (not known by any persons outside that company) by directors or staff in order to profit in share dealings. Such actions constitute a criminal offence.

## insolvency
The inability of a person or company to settle debts when they become payable.

## Institute of Financial Planning (IFP) [UK]
A professional body dedicated to building and maintaining the profession of Financial Planning for the benefit of consumers in the UK. It aims to achieve this by: promoting the profession and practice of financial planning; encouraging education in the theory and practice of financial planning; establishing a register of certified practitioners who have achieved the Certified Financial Planner (CFP); establishing practical and ethical standards.

## institution
An organisation which invests the monies of its own investors. Such organisations are typically banks, insurance companies, mutual funds, unit trusts and pension funds etc and are very influential in the investment market due to the large sums of money at their disposal.

## insurable interest
A term which means that any person entering into an insurance contract must stand to lose financially following the loss or damage of an insured item, or an insured event. For example a person may insure his/her property and contents since a financial loss would be incurred if damage were to be sustained.

## insurance
A contract in which payment of premiums covers the *insured* against something which may, or may not occur. For example *motor insurance* covers the insured against accidents which may occur. In the UK insurance is differentiated from assurance (life assurance) which is protection against something which will inevitably occur.

### insurance broker
A person specialising in insurance matters and who gives advice on the subject as well as arranging cover. Remuneration would normally be by way of commission from the *insurer*.

### insurance policy
The document which specifies the details and conditions of cover of an insurance contract together with the premium payable.

### insurance premium
The amount payable by the *insured* in return for indemnification against specified risks.

### insurance premium tax (IPT) [UK]
A tax imposed on certain general insurance premiums. The rates are currently (2009) 17.5% on travel insurance and 5% on other types of general insurance. There is no IPT on long-term insurance such as *life assurance* and *permanent health insurance*.

### insured
A person or company acquiring insurance.

### insurer
An authorised company which provides insurance.

### intangible assets
Assets which are non-physical in form, that is, which cannot be seen. Examples are patents, goodwill, trademarks and copyrights. See also *tangible assets*.

### inter bank clearing
The process of payment clearance between two banks.

## inter branch clearing

The process of payment clearance between two branches of the same bank.

## interest

The charge made for borrowed money. For example if a bank (the lender) lends money to a customer (the borrower) a charge will be made which is dependent on the *interest rate* in existence at the time of the loan. If a loan is made of say $1,000 at a rate of 10% per year, the interest payable is $100 per year. This does not take into consideration the repayment of the $1,000. The rate of interest may be variable or fixed. See simple interest. See *compound interest*.

## interest in possession

The legal right to receive income from or to occupy trust property.

## interest only mortgage

A *mortgage* where regular payments (usually monthly) only meet the interest requirements. The interest rate is usually variable and linked to prevailing rates but can be fixed for a given period. The capital amount outstanding remains approximately the same and the borrower will need to make additional provision for repaying this amount at the end of the term of the loan.

## interest rate

The percentage rate at which *interest* is charged on a loan for a period of one year.

## interest rate swap

An arrangement whereby two parties agree to exchange responsibilities for fixed and variable rates of interest repayments. For example company A may require a fixed interest rate so as to be sure as to what the repayments will be. However company B may prefer a variable rate although it can obtain a fixed rate below that of company A perhaps by 2%. The two companies then exchange loans with, for example, company A taking on the fixed loan and paying 1% to company B. Thus both companies obtain the type of loan each requires at a cheaper rate than that directly available from a bank.

### interim
A term which means in the meantime. See interim bonus and interim dividend.

### interim bonus [UK]
A bonus declared by life companies when maturity of a *with profits* policy or death of the *assured* occurs between normal *bonus declaration* dates.

### interim dividend
The *dividend* declared before annual earnings are established. In the USA, a dividend is usually paid quarterly. Companies in the UK usually pay two dividends per year, the interim dividend and the *final dividend.* The interim dividend is usually the smaller of the two.

### intermediary
An *agent, broker* or financial institution who can give advice and act as a middle person between a company and a client conducting investment business.

### Internal Revenue Service (IRS) [USA]
The US agency responsible for the collection of federal taxes which include personal and corporate income taxes, excise and gift taxes.

## *intrinsic value*

### International Monetary Fund
A fund formed in the mid 1940s by industrialised countries to stabilise exchange rates, promote international trading and provide short term loans to member countries with *balance of payments* problems.

### international fund [USA]
A *mutual fund* whose portfolio comprises a range of securities from markets around the world.

### International Petroleum Exchange (IPE)
A recognised investment exchange, IPE is Europe's leading energy *futures* and *options* exchange and the second largest in the world. It is the home of the benchmark Brent Crude contracts. provides a highly regulated market place where industry participants can manage their exposure to highly volatile energy prices. The IPE has forged an alliance with the *Chicago Climate Exchange*.

### intestate
The situation which exists when a person dies without making a will. The person is then said to have died intestate. The UK's intestacy rules specify how the estate must be distributed.

### intrinsic value
1. An *options* expression which indicates the difference between the current price of the *underlying instrument* (for example a commodity or equity product) and the *exercise price*. A *call option* has intrinsic value if the exercise price is below that of the underlying instrument and is said to be *in the money*. If the exercise price of a *put option* is below that of the underlying instrument there is no intrinsic value and it is said to be *out of the money*.

2. The difference between the current ordinary share price of a *security* and the *exercise price* of a *warrant*. If the exercise price is below the ordinary share price there is intrinsic value. If the exercise price is above the ordinary share price there is no intrinsic value. There may however be some *time value*.

### invalidity benefit [UK]
A former state benefit payable after the expiry of state *sickness benefit* if a person was still unfit to work. This benefit was replaced by *incapacity benefit* in April 1995.

### inventory
1. A company's finished goods, work in progress and raw materials. In the UK, an alternative to *stock in trade*.
2. An itemised list of an individual's assets.

### investments
The buying for example of shares or stock, shares in *mutual funds*, units in *unit trusts* etc in order to make financial gain. The placing of money with banks and other financial institutions in order to earn *interest* tends to be known as *deposit taking business*. In the UK, the *Financial Services and Markets Act 2000* defines investments to include shares, debentures and other securities such as government securities, certain options and warrants, unit trusts and other forms of collective investment schemes, futures contracts and some long term life insurance contracts. See *investment business*.

### investment bond [UK]
A unit linked single premium whole life assurance policy. Part of the premium gives life cover whilst the balance is invested in unitised funds. Under certain circumstances, since the bond is a life policy, certain tax advantages may be

enjoyed. For example basic rate taxpayers pay no tax on any gain made on the policy; higher rate taxpayers pay only the excess over the basic rate. See *unit linked policy*.

### investment business [UK]
*The Financial Services Act and Markets 2000* defines investment business to include dealing, arranging deals in, managing and advising on investments in addition to the setting up and operation of collective investment schemes. See *investments* and *deposit taking business*.

### investment club
A group of individuals who combine their capital and subsequently decide where investments are made, this usually being on a monthly or quarterly basis. The advantage of these clubs is that members' funds are invested in a range of securities thus reducing risk and fees. There are also the educational advantages. In the US, advice for starting up such clubs is available from the *National Association of Investors Corporation* in Michigan. For the UK see *ProShare*.

### investment company [USA]
A company which invests the funds of small private investors in a range of securities. This enables fund shareholders to partake in ownership of a diversified portfolio of shares. Investment companies are classified as either *open end* (*mutual fund*) or *closed end* (*investment trust*).

### investment grade [USA]
The description of a highly regarded bond with a rating of AAA to BBB.

### investment income
Income, paid from an investment, such as dividends and interest.

## Investment Management Regulatory Organisation (IMRO) [UK]

Formerly a *Self Regulating Organisation* with responsibility for regulating investment fund management. Now superseded by the Financial Services Authority.

## investment trust

A company which invests its shareholders' funds in the shares of other companies. This enables small private investors to participate in ownership of a diversified portfolio of shares. Investment trusts are *closed end funds*, that is, there are a fixed number of shares in circulation, normally traded on a stock exchange, where prices are governed by what the market is prepared to pay, that is, by supply and demand. The value of a trust's assets less its liabilities is known as the *net asset value (NAV)*. When the share price of a trust is less than the NAV per share it is said to trade at a *discount*. This may be because the shares are not particularly in demand. If however the share price is higher than the NAV, the trust is said to trade at a *premium*. There is a wide variety of investment trusts available in which to invest with differing objectives.

## Investors Compensation Scheme (ICS) [UK]

Former compensation scheme for investors. Now incorporated in the *Financial Services Compensation Scheme*.

## invoice

A document, issued by a person or company, indicating to the recipient the amount of money owed to that person or company for goods and/or services supplied. When a number of transactions occur during a month between companies regularly, it is usual for a summary of invoices submitted to be tendered on a *statement* at the end of the month for overall settlement.

## irredeemable securities [UK]
Securities, such as some *debentures* (perpetual debentures) and certain government loan stock (Consols) which do not have a redemption date that is there is no date specified for repayment of capital.

## issue
1. The number of shares of a company on sale to the public at a given time.
2. A child mentioned in a will.

## issue price
The price at which a company's shares are offered to the market for the first time. When they begin to be traded, the *market price* may be above or below the issue price. See *new issue*.

## issued share capital
The amount of *authorised share capital* that shareholders have actually subscribed to a company for share ownership.

## issuing house
A financial *institution* such as a *merchant bank* which provides its services to launch the shares of new companies on a stock exchange. It also ensures that the *listing* of such *issues* complies with exchange regulations.

# J

**jobber [UK]**
A dealer in shares prior to the event known as *Big Bang* in October 1986. Jobbers dealt with investors only via stockbrokers who advised their clients on share transactions. After Big Bang, jobbers were replaced by *market makers*.

**joint account**
Typically a bank or brokerage account in the names of two (or more) persons. Arrangements can be made such that either individual or all signatures are required when drawing checks/cheques.

**joint and several liability**
An undertaking by a group of two or more persons to be responsible for any liability which may exist after any member or members have failed to meet their obligations. For example if a group of four persons enter into a joint and several liability on a bank loan, then in the event of two of the members reneging on their obligations the remaining two members become fully responsible for the repayment of the loan.

**joint liability**
The legal liability of two or more persons for claims against or debts incurred by them jointly. If three persons have joint liability and are indebted to another party, they may only be sued as a group and not individually.

### joint life assurance [UK]
An assurance policy usually taken out on two lives, typically husband and wife. The *sum assured* is normally payable at the event of the first death, but joint whole of life policies payable on second death are appropriate to cover liability to inheritance tax.

### joint ownership
Equal ownership of property by two or more persons. In the event of the death of one of the owners, title passes to the survivor (or survivors in equal amounts).

### joint life annuity
Income usually relevant to two persons (for example man and wife) which continues until the death of the first person only.

### joint life and survivor annuity
Income usually relevant to two persons (for example man and wife) which continues until the death of the second person.

### joint tax return [USA]
A tax return completed and signed by two persons, usually a husband and wife. They have equal responsibility for taxes due. Filing a joint tax return can result in lower taxes than filing individually.

### joint tenants
Two or more persons owning property. In the event of the death of one of the tenants, the property passes to the survivor(s).

**judgement**
A ruling by a court of law. An example is the ordering of a court to a person to settle a debt to another.

**jumbo certificate of deposit [USA]**
A certificate of deposit with a denomination of $100,000 and above. They are usually purchased by large institutions such as banks and insurance companies.

**junk bonds**
Bonds which offer high rates of interest but with correspondingly higher risk attached to the capital. In the US they carry a credit rating of BB and below.

### knock for knock agreement

### kangaroos
A term for Australian shares with emphasis on mining, tobacco and land companies.

### Keogh pension plan [USA]
A *tax deferred* retirement savings plan for the self employed. Contributions are based on a percentage of earned income and are tax deductible. Investment growth is tax deferred until the withdrawal of capital.

### key person insurance
An insurance policy taken out on the life of a company executive or senior employee whose death would cause significant loss to the company. In the event of such a death the proceeds of the policy would be payable to the company.

### kiddie tax [USA]
A tax imposed on the investment income (dividends, interest and capital gains) of dependent children where such income exceeds a certain level. The tax level is the parents' highest rate.

### knock for knock agreement
Although it currently rarely applies, this is a motor insurance term describing an agreement between insurance companies where each pays the claims of its own clients following an accident. This principle applies irrespective of blame and

### *know your customer*

seeks to save time and expense. One of the parties involved in such circumstances may however seek to sue the other and if successful may claim from the other's insurers.

### know your customer [USA] know your client [UK]
The ethical principle relating to broker dealers and *financial advisers* that all reasonable steps have been taken to gather sufficient relevant financial and personal information regarding the customer and that subsequent investment recommendations will take full account of that information.

### Krugerrand
A coin minted in South Africa containing one ounce of pure gold and originally intended as an investment item.

### landlord
A property owner who rents it to another party called a tenant.

### lapse
In insurance terminology, a policy is deemed to have lapsed when the policyholder fails to pay the renewal premiums. Also, it may be that the insurers do not invite renewal.

### lapsed option [USA]
The expiry of an *option* without being exercised by the holder. In the UK this is known as *abandonment*.

### lasting power of attorney [UK]
A *power of attorney* which, subject to conditions and safeguards continues in force even after the maker of the lasting power of attorney (the 'donor') may become mentally incapable of conducting his/her affairs. This replaced the formerly-used enduring power of attorney, although existing enduring powers of attorney can remain in force. Equivalent to durable power of attorney in the USA.

### last trading day
An expression used in *futures* and *options* trading which refers to the last day for trading in a *contract* for a particular delivery or expiry month.

### late charge [USA]
A charge imposed by a lender to a borrower when the borrower fails to make payment on the due date.

## laundering
The manipulation of money obtained in a wrongful manner, for example theft, so as to make it seem to have originated from a lawful source. An example is to pay the unlawful money into an overseas bank and subsequently transfer back to the country of origin.

## Law Society [UK]
The professional body for solicitors in England and Wales. Its aims and objectives are defined in the 1845 Royal Charter as having a responsibility to promote a 'professional improvement and facilitate the acquisition of legal knowledge'. The primary responsibility is to train and support solicitors to ensure they 'offer access to justice for all'. Also to enhance the reputation of the legal system by developing and maintaining standards in training and continuing education, admission of solicitors, professional ethics and investigation of complaints.

## LCH.Clearnet
Formerly the London Clearing House, its primary role is to act as central counterparty for trades conducted on the futures and options markets in London. Once LCH.Clearnet has registered a trade, it becomes the buyer to every member who sells and seller to every member who buys, thereby guaranteeing that the financial obligations of trades are met. It clears a broad range of asset classes including securities, exchange traded derivatives and interest rate swaps. LCH.Clearnet is a *Recognised Clearing House* under the regulatory supervision of the *Financial Services Authority (FSA)*.

## lease
A contract in which the legal owner of property or other asset agrees to another person using that property or asset in

return for a regular specified payment (known as ***rent***) over a set term. In addition to buildings, other items such as cars and computers are often leased in order to avoid capital costs in the running of a business.

**lease back**
A situation whereby a property is sold by its owner to another person or company on condition that the purchaser leases the property back to the original owner for an agreed ***rent*** over a set term. This enables the original owner to raise capital which can be used for other purposes.

**leasehold land**
Land which is rented from the owner for a specified term under a *lease*. At the expiry of the term the land reverts back to the owner. Under certain circumstances, leaseholders in the UK may have the right to purchase the freehold.

**ledger**
A book in which the accounts of a business are kept. In the UK the main ledgers operating within a business are the ***nominal ledger***, the ***sales ledger*** and the ***purchase ledger***. The nominal ledger contains the nominal accounts which list revenue and operating expenses (for example building costs, vehicles etc) and the real accounts which detail the company's assets and capital. The sales ledger contains the sales accounts of customers and the purchase ledger contains the purchase accounts of suppliers. The sales accounts and purchase accounts are also known as personal accounts. In most businesses in current times such accounting information is stored in computers.

**legacy**
Another term for bequest, that is, the making of a gift by ***will***. There are three main types of legacy. **Pecuniary legacy**: A

gift of a fixed sum of money left for example to an individual or a charity. **Specific legacy**: A gift of a specific item (such as a set of books) left for example to a friend. **Residuary legacy**: A gift consisting of the residue of an estate after all other conditions of the will have been met, or part of such residue.

### legal expenses insurance
Insurance, taken out by individuals or companies for protection against defending civil actions brought about by other individuals or companies or alternatively to pursue them, where legal expenses (for example lawyer's fees) will be incurred.

### legal list [USA]
A list of approved securities in which institutions such as savings banks, life insurance companies and pension funds may invest.

### lender
A person or company that offers to lend money to a borrower for a given period of time. The borrower is obliged to repay the loan either by instalments or single payment together with specified interest.

### lender of last resort
A prime function of a country's central bank. In the USA the lender of last resort is the *Federal Reserve Bank*. In the UK the *Bank of England* provides this role.

### lessee
A person to whom a *lease* is granted, known as a *tenant*.

### lessor
A person who grants a *lease*, known as a landlord.

### letter of intent [USA]
In relation to *mutual funds*, an undertaking by a shareholder to make monthly investment payments for a period of one year. In return, the shareholder qualifies for a reduction in sales fees.

### letter of renunciation
In a *rights issue* of shares, a letter of renunciation is the form attached to an *allotment letter* which the holder completes should he/she wish to transfer entitlement to another person or to renounce his/her rights absolutely.

### letter of wishes
See *memorandum of wishes*.

### letters of administration
An order made by the court empowering the *administrator* to settle the affairs of a deceased person in accordance with his/her *will* where an *executor* has not been named or has predeceased (or fails to act for some other reason) and similarly when a person has died *intestate* that is, a deceased person who has failed to make a will.

### level annuity
See *annuity*.

### level term insurance
See *term life insurance (UK term assurance)*.

### leverage
In the US, the ratio of a company's *long term debt*, typically bonds and preferred stock, to its equity in its capital structure. The greater the long term debt, the greater the leverage. In the UK the term for leverage is *gearing*.

### leveraged buyout (LBO)
The takeover of a company, financed by capital raised by the purchaser by heavy borrowing on the assets of the target company and its own assets.

### liabilities
The debts of a person or company. See *current liabilities*, *long term liabilities*, *contingent liabilities*.

### liability insurance
Insurance against legal liability to pay compensation and court costs where the *insured* has been found negligent in respect of injuries sustained by another person or damage to his/her property.

### lien
The right of an individual to retain possession of the goods of another until the latter fulfils his/her obligations such as the payment of an outstanding debt.

### life insurance [USA] life assurance[UK]
An insurance policy which, in return for the payment of regular premiums, pays a lump sum on the death of the *insured* (UK *life assured*). In the case of *cash value insurance*, in addition to life cover, a savings element provides benefits which are payable before death. In the UK *endowment assurance* provides life cover or a maturity value after a specified term, whichever is the sooner.

### life of another [UK]
A life assurance policy taken out on the life of another person by the policyholder. For example a man may take out a life assurance policy (where he is the policyholder that is, the *assured*) on the life of his wife (the *life assured*) in order to cover various expenditures (for example a nanny for children) should the death of his wife occur.

## lifetime mortgage [UK]
See *home income plan*.

## limit order
An order to buy (for example shares) up to a maximum price or sell down to a minimum price. For example an investor may place a limit order to buy shares at $12 where the current price was say $15 and falling. If the price levels at $13 and goes up again the order would not be placed. Similarly if the price fell to $12 or below, the investor's order would be placed and the maximum he/she would pay would be $12.

## limit price
The maximum buying price or minimum selling price a client is prepared to respectively pay or accept for shares or commodities etc.

## limited company [UK]
A company whose shareholders' maximum liability is limited to their share capital in the event of winding up.

## limited liability
The principle that the liability of shareholders for debts of a corporation or limited company is limited to the nominal value of their shares.

## limited liability partnership [UK]
A partnership in which all partners have limited personal liability, each partner's liability being restricted to the amount that he/she invested in the business.

## limited partnership
A partnership comprising a general partner and limited partners. The general partner operates the partnership and is fully liable for the debts of the firm. Limited partners receive

some of the profits and have no influence in management. However their liabilities are limited to their original investment.

### liquid assets
A company's cash plus assets which can readily be converted into cash.

### liquid market
A market in which large quantities of shares (or commodities etc) are being bought and sold thereby making trading straightforward. This situation will also reduce the *spread* that is, the difference between the buying and selling price of shares.

### liquidation
The sale of a company's assets to settle as far as possible the debts to its *creditors* prior to its winding up. Any cash left over is distributed to its shareholders.

### liquidator
An official appointed to supervise the *liquidation* of a company.

### liquidity
The ease with which assets can be sold to realise cash.

### liquidity ratio
The ratio of *liquid assets* (current assets less stocks) to *current liabilities*. A measure of a company's ability to pay its short-term debts.

### listed company [UK]
A company that has satisfied the requirements for its shares to be listed on a *Recognised Investment Exchange (RIE)*. In

the case of the ***London Stock Exchange***, a company which has obtained permission for its shares to be admitted to the ***Daily Official List***.

### listed firm [USA]
A company whose stock is traded on a leading stock exchange such as the ***New York Stock Exchange*** or ***American Stock Exchange***.

### listed securities
Securities such as shares, stocks, bonds etc which are quoted on a leading stock exchange such as the ***New York Stock Exchange (NYSE)*** and the ***American Stock Exchange*** in the USA and the ***London Stock Exchange*** in the UK.

### listing requirements [USA] listing particulars [UK]
Details which a company is obliged to publish about itself together with any securities it issues before it obtains a listing on a recognised stock exchange.

### litigation
The process of a person or company taking legal action against another.

### Lloyds
The oldest and largest insurance market. Members are Lloyds brokers and syndicates of Lloyds underwriters forming a corporation. Business is obtained via Lloyds brokers dealing with the public which is underwritten by syndicates of Lloyds underwriters so organised as to spread risk. Members of syndicates are known as Names and must deposit a substantial sum of money (with unlimited risk attached) before acceptance. The main business is in marine insurance although virtually all other insurance (with the exception of life assurance) is covered.

### load fund [USA]
A *mutual fund* in which shares are sold by a broker to an investor for a sales commission in return for which fund details would be explained.

### loading
1. A term for administration charges imposed by *institutions* on mutual funds, unit trusts and pension plans. See *front end load* and *back end load*.
2. An addition to the premium for an insurance policy where extra risk is involved.

### loan
An advance of money from a lender to a borrower over a period of time. The borrower is obliged to repay the loan either at intervals during or at the end of the loan period together with interest.

### loan account
An *account*, opened for a customer by a bank, following the granting of a loan. The amount of the loan is credited to the customer's *current account* and similarly debited to the loan account. An arrangement is subsequently made for the customer to repay the loan, usually over a stated period of time, with interest additionally being paid on the outstanding amount.

### loan capital [UK]
That part of a company's capital structure which is raised by loans. Such loans (typically *debentures*) are usually over a stated period of time and pay fixed interest to the person making the loan. At the end of the period the capital is repaid. This contrasts with *share capital* where shareholders are entitled to a proportion of the company's profits usually by way of *dividends*. See *gearing*.

## loan interest
Interest payable on a loan. See *interest*.

## loan protection policy
An insurance policy in which the insured pays regular premiums in return for insurance against being unable to repay a loan due to accident, sickness or unemployment. In such an event the policy pays a benefit to assist the insured in making the repayments.

## loan stock [UK]
A security bearing a fixed rate of interest. The capital (the amount loaned) is repaid after a given period of time.

## local authority investment
A bond issued by a local authority in order to raise capital for its budget.

## local taxes
In the USA, taxes paid by an individual to a local state or county. These are deductible on the person's federal tax return. In the UK the nearest equivalent is the tax paid by houseowners to their local council (*council tax*). There is no tax relief on such payments but reductions can be claimed from the local council in cases where houseowners receive low income.

## London Bullion Market
A two way market place in which investors can sell or buy both gold and silver. *Market makers* mainly quote prices in US dollars per troy ounce for *spot* and forward delivery. *Forward prices* and *options* quoted by market makers enable producers and industrial consumers to *hedge* their future commitments and provide access for investors and speculators.

## London Bullion Market Association

**London Bullion Market Association (LBMA)**
An Association which represents the interests of the participants of the *London Bullion Market*. One of its primary tasks is to ensure that refiners of gold and silver meet the required standards of quality before their inclusion in the Market's Good Delivery lists. Investment business including derivatives is regulated by the *Financial Services Authority*. Other business is covered by the London Code of Conduct for Non-Investment Products, drawn up in conjunction with the *Bank of England*.

**London Clearing House**
See *LCH.Clearnet*

**London Commodity Exchange**
A former *futures* and *options* exchange, dealing in soft commodities including cocoa, sugar, coffee, wheat, barley and potatoes, it merged in 1996 with the *London International Financial Futures and Options Exchange* (LIFFE) where trades of the merged company are guaranteed by *LCH.Clearnet*.

**London Inter Bank Offered Rate (LIBOR)**
The rate of interest at which banks will lend money to each other. In practice there is a range of rates for terms from overnight to 12 months.

**London International Financial Futures and Options Exchange (LIFFE)**
A *futures* and *options* exchange which originally dealt solely in financial instruments including equities (shares), government bonds, indices (such as the FT-SE 100 Index) interest rates and a wide range of currencies. In 1996, LIFFE merged with the then *London Commodity Exchange* with unified administration and exchange systems. All trades

## London Stock Exchange

of the merged exchange are guaranteed by *LCH.Clearnet*. LIFFE is a *Recognised Investment Exchange (RIE)*, regulated by the *Financial Services Authority (FSA)*.

### London Metal Exchange (LME)
An international market for the trading of non-ferrous metals, it offers futures and options contracts for aluminium, copper, nickel, tin, zinc and lead plus two regional aluminium alloy contracts. In 2005 the Exchange launched the world's first futures contracts for plastics. LCH.Clearnet acts as guarantor to trades conducted between members. The LME is a *Recognised Investment Exchange (RIE)*, regulated by the *Financial Services Authority (FSA)*.

### London Securities and Derivatives Exchange (OMLX)
An integrated exchange and *clearing house* for *futures* and *options derivatives*, owned by the Swedish-based OM Group and based mainly on the Swedish and Norwegian equity markets. Products include futures and options on the OMX Swedish equity index (the 30 most liquid shares traded on the Stockholm Stock Exchange), the OBX Norwegian equity index (the 25 most traded stocks on the Oslo Stock Exchange), Swedish equity futures and options and Norwegian equity futures and options. OMLX is a *Recognised Investment Exchange (RIE)*, regulated by the *Financial Services Authority (FSA)*.

### London Stock Exchange
The UK market-place for the trading of *listed securities* (shares, government stocks [gilts], bonds etc). It maintains market rules and regulations and provides a range of services for market users. The Exchange provides a highly active and efficient market for trading in a wide range of securities, including UK and international equities, debt, *real estate investment trusts* (reits), fixed interest securities. TradElect,

*long*

the Exchange's electronic trading system executes over 600,000 trades daily. Trading in the various securities is by way of *market makers* who are required to make buying and selling prices for the securities in which they are registered. In order for a company to be admitted to the Exchange it must make application for a place on the *'Official List'*. This involves providing extensive data regarding its financial status and trading history etc. The London Stock Exchange is a *Recognised Investment Exchange* under the regulatory supervision of the *Financial Services Authority (FSA)*.

**long**
See *long position*.

**long bond [USA]**
In the USA, a bond with a maturity of more than ten years. Also the US 30 year Treasury bond.

**long position**
The purchase of a security, commodity or financial instrument (for example, currencies etc) in the belief that the price will increase. The purchaser would then hope to sell it at a higher price and thus make a profit. See *short position*.

**long term debt [USA]**
Debt liabilities due in one year or more.

**long term care insurance**
The planning, by way of suitable insurance, for covering partially or in full, the cost of long term care in old age. The place of care may be the insured's own residence or a nursing home. In order to claim benefit, the *insured* must be disabled to the extent that he/she is unable to perform a specified number of daily activities such as washing, dressing and eating/drinking.

### long term gain [USA]
A gain on a capital asset relating to a holding period of more than one year.

### long term liabilities
Debts of a company which are not due for repayment in the next accounting period.

### longs [UK]
1. *Redeemable gilts* or bonds with a *redemption date* beyond fifteen years.
2. Securities (for example, shares), commodities or financial instruments (for example, indices, currencies etc) held in a *long position*.

### loss of income insurance [USA]
Insurance in which the *insured* is covered against loss of income.

### lot
An alternative expression for contract in *futures* and *options* trading. See *contract 2*.

### low cost endowment assurance
See *endowment assurance*.

### low start endowment assurance
See *endowment assurance*.

### lower earnings limit [UK]
That level of income at which employees start to pay *Class 1 National Insurance contributions*.

### lower rate tax [UK]
The lowest rate of income tax in the UK, currently 10%. Applicable only to investment income; not applicable to earned income.

**lump sum**
A sum of money paid in a single instalment.

**luxury tax [USA]**
A tax on goods considered to be luxury items.

## M0, M1, M2, M3, M4
See *money supply*.

## macroeconomics
The study of a country's economy using such elements as unemployment, price levels, government spending, interest rates, national productivity etc and the influence of government policy on them. See *microeconomics*.

## maintenance payments [UK]
Money paid by a divorced or separated man to his ex-wife to assist her with living expenses. (In unusual circumstances payment could be made by the wife to her ex-husband). From the taxation point of view, maintenance may be enforceable following a court order, or voluntary. Where maintenance is enforceable the recipient will not be liable for tax, but the person making the payments can claim limited tax relief. For voluntary payments, the recipient is not liable for tax and the person making the payments cannot claim tax relief.

## making a market
Being able and willing to buy or sell a security as a dealer. In the USA an exchange dealer is known as a *specialist* and an over the counter dealer is called a *market maker*. See *making a price*.

## making a price
In the UK, a term used on the *London Stock Exchange* which refers to the obligation of a *market maker* to quote a broker both a price at which he/she is willing to purchase

a *security* and a price at which he/she is willing to sell. The market maker would not normally be aware as to whether the enquirer wishes to buy or sell but once the prices have been given they must be honoured if the broker wishes to deal.

**managed account**
An investment account, managed by the investment department of a bank for a client.

**managed fund**
A *unit linked* fund managed by a *life assurance* company. The fund is invested in a wide range of securities so as to keep risk to a minimum.

**management charges**
Charges made by the managers of, for example, a *mutual fund* or *unit trust* which include for investment management and administration costs etc.

**mandate**
An official order from an authority to implement an action.

**mandatory quote period**
A term used on the *London Stock Exchange* which refers to the period of time during which *market makers* in a security are obliged to display their prices. For SEAQ (*Stock Exchange Automated Quotations* system), the period is from 8.30am to 4.30pm.

**margin**
1. The difference between the cost price of a product and the selling price. See *gross margin*.
2. In securities trading, the amount deposited with a broker in order to obtain credit for purchase of a security

(securities). The margin is the price of a security less credit advanced by the broker.
3. The difference between a ***market maker***'s buying and selling prices. Also known as ***spread***.
4. In futures trading, the amount which must be deposited by an investor prior to trading.

**margin account**
An account with a broker where a client is able to purchase securities on credit after ***margin*** has been deposited.

**margin call**
A demand from a broker to a client to provide more funds to bring a ***margin account*** balance up to a required level.

**margin securities**
Securities which may be bought or sold on ***margin***. In the USA, an approved list of margin securities is published by the Federal Reserve Board.

**marginal tax rate**
The additional tax paid on each unit (for example dollar or pound) increase of taxable income.

**market**
1. A place for the buying and selling of goods and services.
2. A gathering of traders within an exchange, where securities are bought and sold, for example the ***New York Stock Exchange*** or the ***London Stock Exchange***.

**market capitalisation**
The approximate value of a company which is calculated by multiplying its total issued shares by the current share price. This value will constantly change in accordance with any increase or decrease in the share price.

## marital deduction [USA]
The provision for tax free transference of property between spouses irrespective of value. In the UK transfers between spouses are free from *inheritance tax*.

## market maker
A dealer in securities who is obliged to offer buying and selling prices for those securities in which he/she deals. These prices must be honoured if a broker decides to deal. In the USA, 'market maker' is the term often given to a dealer in the over the counter market. An exchange (for example the New York Stock Exchange) dealer is known as a *specialist*. In the UK, the term 'market maker' is given to those dealing on a main exchange such as the London Stock Exchange.

## market order
An order to buy or sell *securities* or *commodities* at the best price with immediate effect.

## market price
The price for a security. There is however a market price for selling and a market price for buying and when quoted in newspapers etc the value is usually an average of these. In the UK, this is also known as the *mid price*. The difference between the buying and selling prices is known as the *spread* or *margin*.

## Mastercard
An international payment services and card scheme.

## maturity
The capital repayment date of a *bond*. Also the end of the term of a *cash value insurance* policy (endowment assurance policy in the UK).

## means test
An appraisal of a person's income and assets to establish if he/she qualifies for state benefits.

## medical insurance
See *health insurance* (USA). See *private medical insurance* (UK).

## mediums [UK]
*Redeemable gilts* or bonds with a *redemption date* (maturity date) between five and fifteen years.

## medium term bond [USA]
A bond with a maturity between two and ten years. In the UK medium term bonds are popularly known as *mediums*.

## member bank [USA]
A bank which is a member of the *Federal Reserve System*.

## member firm [USA]
A brokerage firm that has a minimum of one member on a stock exchange whereby the membership is in the name of an individual and not the firm.
[UK] A trading firm of brokers or market makers which is a member of the *London Stock Exchange*. Member firms may deal in shares on behalf of itself or on behalf of its clients.

## memorandum of association [UK]
Those details which a company, when formed, must submit to the *Registrar of Companies* together with its *articles of association*. They include company name, registered office, object, authorised share capital and a statement of limited liability etc.

## memorandum of wishes (letter of wishes)
A memorandum or letter addressed to the *executor*s of a *will* by the *testator* (feminine testatrix), that is, the maker of the will, specifying additional wishes to be carried out. For example a woman may leave her jewellery to her executor with a letter of wishes requesting that they pass certain items to named individuals.

## merchant
A trader who purchases goods for resale in home or foreign markets.

## merchant bank
A bank which offers a range of services including the raising of capital for companies, advice on international trading, takeovers and mergers and flotations etc. Many UK retail ("High Street") banks have subsidiaries or departments providing similar services.

## microeconomics
The study of economic elements at the level of the household or the company. Persons within a household are primarily concerned with employment prospects and how taxation affects their income. Companies are mainly concerned with product costs and operating expenses etc. See *macroeconomics*.

## middle price
See *mid price*.

## mid price
The average of the *bid price* and *offer price* of a security.

## minimum contributions
See *appropriate personal pension plan*.

## minimum maintenance [USA]
The minimum amount of equity which must be kept in a margin account as specified by the New York Stock Exchange, the National Association of Securities Dealers and brokerage firms.

## minimum quote size
A *London Stock Exchange* term which refers to the minimum number of shares in which market makers must display prices on the *SEAQ* for those securities for which they are registered.

## monetary policy
The control of the *money supply* and interest rates by a government in order to achieve its economic objectives, in particular the restraining of *inflation*. See fiscal policy.

## Monetary Policy Committee (MPC) [UK]
The nine-member committee at the Bank of England that meets monthly to set the Bank's base rate (*repo rate*) with the overall aim of achieving the government's inflation target.

## money
A medium of exchange usually consisting of coins and bank notes, plus deposits in banks and building societies.

## money broker
A type of *agent* who arranges short term loans between banks (which are seeking to lend money) and borrowers such as institutions. The money broker is not involved in the process of lending/borrowing but merely acts as an intermediary earning a commission.

## money laundering
See *laundering*.

## money market

A market in which money and other *liquid assets* such as *bills of exchange* and *Treasury bills* can be lent and borrowed in order to satisfy the short term (from overnight to several months) *cash flow* requirements of banks and other institutions. Where personal investors have large sums of money to deposit, they can also gain access to the money market via the commercial banks.

## money purchase scheme (defined contributions scheme)

A *pension* scheme in which the benefits will be dependent on contributions to and growth of the fund and the fund manager's costs. See *occupational pension* and *personal pension*.

## money supply

The total amount of money in an economy at a given time. Central banks regularly publish measures of the money supply (known as monetary aggregates).

[USA] Since 2005, the Federal Reserve has published two monetary aggregates. **M1**: currency plus money in checking accounts; **M2**: the components of M1 plus savings accounts, money market accounts and certain other deposits.

[UK] The Bank of England publishes two monetary aggregates. **M0**: sterling notes and coins in circulation outside the Bank of England including those held in tills of banks and building societies plus banks' operational deposits with the Bank of England. Also known as narrow money; **M4**: the components of M0 plus all sterling deposits at UK private sector monetary financial institutions. Also known as broad money.

[EU] The European Central Bank publishes three monetary aggregates. **M1**: Currency and overnight deposits; **M2**: the components of M1 plus deposits; **M3**: the components of M2 plus repurchase agreements, money market funds shares/units and debt securities up to 2 years.

## money transmission
The process of transferring funds and making payments.

## mortgage
A loan whereby the borrower (the mortgagor) offers a property and land as *security* to the lender (the mortgagee) until the loan is repaid. Repayments of the loan are usually made on a monthly basis over a long period of time, typically 25 years. In the UK, the most common forms of mortgage are the *repayment mortgage* and the *interest only mortgage*.

## mortgage backed security [USA]
A security, backed by a pool of mortgages, whereby the shareholder receives payments based on the interest and principal paid on the underlying mortgages.

## mortgage broker [USA]
A person or company engaged in the arrangement of mortgages for buyers. The broker is usually paid a commission by the lender.

## mortgage indemnity guarantee protection
An additional one off payment, made by the borrower of a mortgage (the mortgagor), which, via an insurance policy, protects the lender (such as a bank) when repossessing a property where the sale price is less than the mortgage outstanding. Any such shortfall will be claimed by the lender off the policy. In the UK this payment must be described to the borrower as a higher lending charge.

## mortgage interest deduction [USA]
An allowable federal tax deduction for the annual interest paid on a mortgage.

### mortgage interest relief at source (MIRAS) [UK]
Former scheme under which interest paid on the first £30,000 of a *mortgage* qualified for *income tax* relief. Withdrawn in 2000.

### mortgage payment protection insurance
An accident, sickness and unemployment policy designed to cover mortgage repayments for (typically) up to two years.

### mortgage protection assurance [UK]
Decreasing term assurance designed to pay off the outstanding balance of a repayment mortgage on the death of the life assured (generally the *mortgagor*). The sum assured decreases over time in line with the outstanding balance.

### mortgagee
A company or institution such as a bank or building society (that is, the lender) which advances a loan which is secured by a property and the land on which it is built.

### mortgagor
A person or company who takes out a loan and offers a property and the land on which it is built as security.

### motor insurance [UK]
The insurance of motor vehicles covering damage or loss and liabilities for injuries to other persons and damage to property. It is a legal requirement that drivers are insured against *third party* claims that is, *third party insurance*. Under this type of insurance, if it is proved that the insured is the cause of an accident, the insurance company will only pay for injury or repairs for damage to the property of the third party. A variant of this is *third party fire and theft insurance* which is basically third party insurance plus additional cover if the insured's vehicle is damaged by fire or if stolen. For a

somewhat higher premium, comprehensive insurance gives additional cover to the *insured* including damage to his/her vehicle, personal effects and overseas travel etc. Known as *automobile insurance* in the USA.

### Motor Insurers' Bureau (MIB) [UK]
An organisation formed in 1946 which provides a means of compensating victims of road accidents caused by uninsured or untraceable drivers. Persons who are the victims of accidents caused by uninsured or untraced motorists may claim for bodily injury and property damage (for untraced motorists, property damage only applies to accidents since 2003).

### municipal bond [USA]
A bond issued by a state or local government often to pay for a special project such as a highway. In certain cases, interest is tax exempt.

### municipal bond insurance [USA]
An insurance policy which guarantees a mutual bond in the case of default, issued by private insurers.

### municipal note [USA]
A municipal debt obligation with a maturity of two years or less.

### mutual company
See *mutual organisation*.

### mutual fund [USA]
A collective investment scheme, operated by an *investment company*, which enables small private investors to partake in ownership of a diversified portfolio of shares, bonds and other securities. It is known as an *open end* fund since there

is no fixed amount of *capital* in the fund. Funds are managed by professional fund managers who invest in securities to achieve the trust's objectives such as capital growth, income or a combination of both. Shares purchased from brokers are called *load funds* and those purchased direct from the fund company are called *no load funds*. Shares when sold are redeemed at their *net asset value*. There is a wide range of funds with a variety of objectives available in which to invest including capital growth and income. Similar to a *unit trust* in the UK.

### mutual fund custodian [USA]
A commercial bank or trust company that safeguards securities held by a mutual fund.

### mutual organisation
An organisation which is owned by its members (in the case of an insurance company by its policyholders), that is, there are no shareholders. Members receive a share in the profits of the organisation.

### mutual savings bank [USA]
A savings bank which is owned by its depositors.

**National Association of Investors Corporation**

**naked**
An expression describing the position of the *writer* of an *option* which is not covered by an opposite position in the *underlying instrument* (for example shares, commodities etc).

**narrow market**
A market in which the trading of shares is only light. Slight movement in activity can result in exaggerated price fluctuations.

**narrow money**
Another name for M1 in the USA and M0 in the UK (see *money supply*).

**Nasdaq**
The first electronic stock market created (in 1971), using computers and telecommunications to trade shares rather than a traditional trading floor. Nasdaq was founded by the National Association of Securities Dealers (NASD). It is the largest electronic screen-based stock market in the USA with well over 3,000 companies listed. It is owned and run by the NASDAQ-OMX Group and is regulated by the *Securities and Exchange Commission*.

**National Association of Investors Corporation (NAIC) [USA]**
Also known as BetterInvesting, it is a Michigan-based non-profit organization whose aims are to advise *investment clubs* and to teach individuals how to become successful long-term investors.

## National Association of Securities Dealers (NASD) [USA]
See *Nasdaq*. Formerly a self-regulatory organisation for the US securities industry and once the owner of the *Nasdaq* exchange. Merged with the New York Stock Exchange's regulation committee to form *Financial Industry Regulatory Authority* (FINRA).

## National Credit Union Administration [USA]
An independent federal agency which supervises federal credit unions and insures members deposits.

## national debt
The debt of a government in respect of its borrowing from its own population and from overseas bodies.

## National Girobank
See *Girobank*.

## National Insurance [UK]
A form of taxation on earned income, payable by employees, employers and the self employed, which is notionally to fund state benefits including pensions, sickness, unemployment and maternity. It is part of the state's social security system and ultimately controlled by the Department for Work and Pensions. See *Benefits Agency*.

## National Insurance (NI) Contributions [UK]
There are currently four categories of contributions: Class 1, Class 2, Class 3 and Class 4.
**Class 1**: Employees earning above the *lower earnings limit* pay contributions at a rate dependent on their income and whether they are contracted in or out of *S2P*. Contributions at the full rate are made up to the *upper earnings limit*, with a small additional rate payable on earnings above this limit.

## National Savings Stock Register

In addition to employees' contributions, employers must pay Class 1 contributions on all the employees' earnings.

**Class 2**: Self employed persons pay flat rate Class 2 contributions provided profits are above a certain level.

**Class 3**: These are voluntary contributions which can make up for unpaid contributions.

**Class 4**: Self employed persons also pay a percentage of profits made between given limits, with a small additional rate on earnings above the higher limit.

### National Insurance Contributions Office [UK]

Formerly the Contributions Office, but now part of HM Revenue & Customs, NICO deals with all aspects of National Insurance contribution payments and records.

### National Savings and Investments (NS&I) [UK]

A variety of savings schemes, backed by the government, in which the public can participate. For tax-free lump sum investment of from 2 to 5 years, there are fixed-interest and index-linked Savings Certificates. Other lump sum investments include Guaranteed Growth Bonds and Guaranteed Income Bonds. Premium Bonds pay no direct interest but offer large and small monthly prizes.

### National Savings Bank [UK]

First opened in 1861 and operated initially through post offices, it became the Department of National Savings in 1969 and *National Savings and Investments* in 1996.

### National Savings Certificates

See *National Savings and Investments*.

### National Savings Stock Register [UK]

A register of government stocks *(gilts)* which can be purchased by the public through the Post Office at favourable rates of commission for moderate purchases and sales. Transactions are conducted by mail and interest is paid gross and is taxable. Despite the name, the Register is now administered by the *Bank of England*.

## negative equity [UK]

A situation where the purchaser of a property has taken out a *mortgage* and some time after the purchase, the value of the property falls below the mortgage amount.

For example, Purchase price of property: £80,000. Deposit: £10,000. Mortgage: £70,000.

If the current sale price were to fall to below £70,000, say to £68,000, a negative equity of £2,000 would exist, that is, in the event of a sale, the property seller would end up owing the provider of the mortgage £2,000. In addition there would be other legal and agents fees to be paid. The original deposit of £10,000 would also be lost.

## negotiable

An instrument, such as a *cheque* or a *bill of exchange*, where the *payee* can transfer the value to another person by inserting that person's name or by signing on the reverse side.

## negotiable instrument

A document, such as a check or bill of exchange by which funds are transferred from one person to another.

## net

The return on investments such as savings accounts and fixed interest securities after deduction of tax.

## net assets

The total *assets* of a company (*current assets* plus *fixed assets*) less its *current liabilities*.

## net asset value (NAV) [USA]
In mutual funds, the net value per share.
**[UK]** The total *assets* of a company less all its *liabilities* including *loan capital* and *preference shares*. Usually expressed in pence per share. For example, assets of a company = £12,000,000, liabilities = £3,000,000, number of ordinary shares = 18,000,000.
NAV = (£12,000,000 - £3,000,000) / 18,000,000 = 50p per share. The term is used particularly when valuing *investment trusts*.

## net income [USA]
Net profit.
Also income received by a person after the deduction of tax. *Gross income* less *tax allowances* = *taxable income*. Net income = Gross income less tax.

## net profit
The *gross profit* of a company (total turnover of products sold less costs to purchase or manufacture) less all other expenses. Net profit is usually expressed before or after tax, that is, *net profit before tax* or *net profit after tax*. Often the 'net' is dispensed with in company accounts.

## net profit after tax (profit after tax)
The net profits of a company after taxation. If applicable, *dividends* are normally paid at this stage.

## net profit before tax (pre tax profit)
The net profits of a company immediately prior to taxation.

## net relevant earnings [UK]
A concept that was applicable before *A-Day* when calculating a self-employed person's maximum permitted contributions to a personal pension.

**net yield**
The *yield* on a security (such as shares, bonds etc) after the deduction of tax.

**new issue**
The offering of a company's shares to the market via a stock exchange for the first time or the issuing of additional shares.

**New York Mercantile Exchange (NYM)**
Following the merger with the Commodity Exchange (*COMEX*) in 1994, the exchange operates two divisions that is, NYMEX which deals in futures and options on a number of products including crude oil, heating oil and platinum and COMEX which deals in futures and options on copper, gold and silver.

**New York Stock Exchange (NYSE)**
The principal stock exchange of the US, located on Wall Street where over 2,000 common and preferred stocks are traded. The exchange is run by NYSE Euronext, a company formed by the merger in 2007 of NYSE with the electronic exchange organisation Euronext.

**Nikkei 225 Index**
An index of the average value of the shares of 225 Japanese companies which reflects share price movement on the Tokyo Stock Exchange. The index is weighted according to price so smaller companies can influence the index as much as the larger ones.

**nil paid**
A new issue of shares where no payment has yet been made. This normally applies following a *rights issue*.

## nil shares
A company's newly issued shares which can normally be transferred on a *renounceable document*.

## no claim discount
A discount awarded to a policy holder when no claims have been made on an insurance policy during the period of insurance, usually one year. It takes the form of a reduction in the renewal premium. The motor insurance business uses this approach extensively and companies will usually increase no claim discounts annually up to a maximum, typically 60%, after four or five years. This method of rewarding policy holders with no claims is sometimes used in *household insurance*.

## no load fund [USA]
A *mutual fund* where investors deal directly with the investment company rather than through a broker. Investors are accordingly not charged a sales commission and the net asset value, bid and offer prices are equal.

## no par value (NPV)
The shares of a company which carry no *nominal price* or *par value*.

## nominal account
An account kept in a *ledger* which itemises revenue and expenditure such as sales and operating costs (building running costs, maintenance of vehicles etc).

## nominal income [USA]
Income which does not take account of changes in the *purchasing power* of the dollar.

### nominal ledger
A ledger which contains the *nominal accounts* and *real accounts* of a company.

### nominal price
The price of a security (stocks, shares, bonds etc) when issued which bears no relation to the *market price*. Also known as face value or par value.

### nominal value
See *nominal price*.

### nominee
A person or company nominated by another to act on his/her behalf regarding the holding of securities. See *street name* and *beneficial owner*.

### nominee account
An account operated on behalf of a person (the *beneficial owner*) for the holding of securities.

### nominee company
A company formed by a bank or other organisation which operates *nominee accounts* that is, the holding of shares for the *beneficial owner*.

### non-contributory pension plan
A pension plan in which an employee does not make contributions. The plan is funded totally by the employer.

### non-forfeiture clause
A clause in a life insurance policy which lays out the conditions under which the policy may remain in force for a limited period if the premium remains unpaid after the expiry of the *days of grace*.

## non-participating life insurance policy [USA]
Life insurance which does not pay dividends.

## non-qualifying life policy [UK]
A life assurance policy which does not satisfy the requirements of HM Revenue & Customs and does not qualify for certain tax relief. See qualifying policy.

## normal market size (NMS) [UK]
The *SEAQ* method of classifying shares on the *London Stock Exchange*. This method replaced the previous alpha, beta, gamma, delta shares system which was a reflection of the order of the most actively traded shares. NMS is a value expressed as a number of shares which is applied to determine the minimum quote size for each share.

## normal retirement age [UK]
The age at which an individual normally retires (60 to 70 for men and 55 to 70 for women). Men qualify for the state pension at 65 and women currently qualify at 60. However the qualifying normal retirement age for women will be increasing to 65 by 2020. For *personal pensions*, stakeholder pensions and retirement annuities, individuals may take retirement between the ages of 50 (55 from 2010) and 75.

## normal trading unit [USA]
The normal size of a securities order. A normal trading unit for shares is 100. Also called a round lot. Known as an odd lots where trades of shares are below 100.

## not negotiable
Words written on a *bill of exchange* or *cheque* which prevents enactment following theft. For example if A writes a cheque to B and marks it 'not negotiable', then in the event that the cheque is stolen by C, it could not be cashed since no one can have a good title to it other than B.

*note*

**note [USA]**
A *debt instrument* whereby the issuer promises repayment on or before a specified date.

**notice of assignment**
See *allocation notice*.

**NYMEX**
The division of the *New York Mercantile Exchange* which deals in crude oil, heating oil and platinum *futures* and *options*.

### occupational pension scheme
A pension scheme operated by a company or organisation for the benefit of its employees. The employer and employee contribute to a fund which grows free of tax during the savings period. There are two main types of pension fund, that is, *defined contributions plan* or *defined benefit plan*. At retirement the employee draws an income which is subject to tax.

### Occupational Pensions Regulatory Authority (OPRA) [UK]
The Authority set up under the Pensions Act 1995 to make *occupational pensions* more secure. Subsequently superseded by the Pensions Regulator following the Pensions Act 2004.

### odd lot [USA]
The trading of securities at lots less than 100, that is, less than the normal unit.

### offer
The price indicated by a seller at which he/she is prepared to sell an item.

### offer for sale
A company's invitation to the public to purchase its shares.

### offer price [USA]
1. The price per share of a *mutual fund*. This is the *net asset value* in a *no load fund*. If a *load fund*, the share price is the net asset value plus a sales charge.

*offer to bid*

2. The price at which a new issue of shares is offered to the public.
[UK] The price at which a *market maker* will sell a security (stocks, shares, bonds etc) or the price at which units can be purchased from the managers of a *unit trust*. See *bid price*.

**offer to bid**
A term often used in the UK which enables an investor to establish the growth of his/her investment. It is a comparison between a previous *offer price* (the price the investor paid) of a *unit trust* and the current *bid price* (the price the investor would receive if units were sold). This comparison allows an investor to see exactly how well his/her investment has performed over the period of time in question (for example, over one, three or five years etc).

**Office of Thrift Supervision (OTS) [USA]**
An agency of the US Treasury Department with responsibility for overseeing the savings and loans industry.

**Official List**
See *Daily Official List*.

**offshore**
The location of a financial institution's subsidiary outside its lawful *domicile*.

**offshore funds**
Assets invested offshore (for example the Bahamas or the Channel Islands) where tax advantages exist. However gains are subject to the taxation rules of an investor's domicile (permanent country of residence).

### Old Lady of Threadneedle Street
A traditional name for the *Bank of England*, located in Threadneedle Street, London.

### Ombudsman [UK]
An independent official appointed to investigate the complaints of individuals against commercial organisations and public bodies. See Financial Ombudsman Service.

### OPAS [UK]
An abbreviation for Occupational Pensions Advisory Service. Renamed the *Pensions Advisory Service* as it now covers all types of pension.

### open end fund
Typically a *mutual fund* or *unit trust* or *open ended investment company (OEIC)*. There is no fixed amount of capital in the fund, that is, there is no limit on the number of shares or units the fund or trust can issue and the volume varies up or down according to the buying and selling activities of the investors.

### open ended investment company (OEIC) [UK]
A collective investment scheme enabling investors to partake in ownership of a diversified portfolio of shares. An OEIC is a form of hybrid between a *unit trust* and an *investment trust*: it is a structured company with investors holding shares rather than units as in a unit trust, but the company is open ended in that it can increase or decrease the number of shares according to demand. The price paid for shares reflects the value of the underlying assets and there is a single price for buying and selling. Commissions and management charges are disclosed separately.

### open interest
The net amount of outstanding *open positions* either *long* or *short* in a given *futures* or *options contract*.

### open outcry
A public auction system used for *futures* trading on the floors of futures exchanges where communication is by way of shouting and hand signs between traders.

### open position
1. An expression used in *futures* trading which refers to a *long* or *short* position which has not been offset by an equal and opposite position. This would make a trader vulnerable to market swings.
2. A position held by a securities dealer in which purchases or sales have been made which respectively are unsold or not covered. The dealer would be exposed to market swings.

### opening purchase
A transaction where a buyer becomes the *holder* of an *option*.

### opening sale
A transaction where the seller of an *option* becomes the *writer*.

### operating costs
Also known as overheads, these are the costs to a company manufacturing a product or providing services which are additional to the direct costs. Examples of operating costs are administration staff and sales staff salaries, motor vehicles and building costs such as electricity and rates etc. Examples of direct costs are production staff wages and costs of materials.

## operating profit
A company's profit after deducting its *operating costs* from *gross profit*.

## operational risk
The risk of loss due to a company's inadequate internal processes or from external events. For banks and other financial institutions, a value must be placed on this risk and included in the assessment of capital adequacy. See *Basel Accord*.

## option
An option gives its *holder* the right but not the obligation to purchase (*call option*) or sell (*put option*) an instrument such as a commodity or a *security* at a specified price on or before a given date.

## ordinary shares [UK]
Also known as equities. In the UK, the most common form of shares where holders are owners in a company. Ordinary shareholders may share in the company's profits by way of a *dividend* if the directors approve such a payout. However it may be that all profits are reinvested in the company so that no dividend is paid. Also dividends may not be payable due to poor results. Holders of ordinary shares will seek to enlarge the capital value of their investment by way of share price increase over the long term. They can also vote on major issues but they are the last in line to be paid in the event of the company being wound up. Similar to *common stock* in the USA.

## organised securities exchange [USA]
A stock exchange where trading of listed securities takes place, such as the *New York Stock Exchange*, as opposed to *over the counter* trading.

## out of the money

1. Either a *call option* where the *exercise price* is above the current price of the *underlying instrument* or a *put option* where the exercise price is below the current price of the underlying instrument.
2. *Warrants* with an exercise price above the market price.

## output tax [UK]

The amount of *value added tax* (VAT) a company adds to the price of its product or service. After deducting *input tax*, the balance must be paid to *HM Revenue & Customs*.

## over the counter (OTC)

The way in which securities are traded by telephone and computer link and not on a listed exchange. Although in the USA the OTC market is regulated by the National Association of Securities Dealers, it is distinctly separate from the *Nasdaq* Stock Market. OTC securities are those not listed on Nasdaq nor any of the national US securities exchanges.

## overbought

A term describing a market in which excessive buying has created an artificially high level. Under these circumstances the market is likely to subsequently fall.

## overcapitalised

A term describing a company which has an excess of capital over what it actually needs. Depending on the ratio between loan capital and share capital, the company will probably be accordingly overloaded with interest and dividend payments.

## overdraft

A facility (usually at a bank or other financial institution) enabling an account holder to go into debit for an agreed amount and often for an agreed time. Since money is usually flowing into and out of the account the balance is continually changing and interest is charged on a daily basis. Compared with a loan which is usually for a fixed period with regular repayments, interest tends to be lower for an agreed overdraft. Where a person overdraws without the agreement of the bank, he/she will probably be liable for either heavy charges or in some cases cheques may not be honoured. In principle an overdraft is liable to be recalled at any time.

**overheads**
See *operating costs*.

**oversold**
A term describing a market in which excessive selling has created an artificially low level. Under these circumstances the market is likely to subsequently rise.

**oversubscribed**
A term referring to an *offer for sale* where applications for shares exceed the number of shares available. Often applications will be scaled down such that a lower number of shares will be received than those requested.

**over the counter market**
A decentralised market of securities. There is no physical trading floor and parties deal directly with one another rather than through an exchange.

**paid in capital**
Capital subscribed by shareholders for a company's stock or shares. In the UK, known as paid up capital.

**paid up policy**
In the USA, a life insurance policy where all premiums have been paid. This may be a policy where premiums are paid for a set number of years after which it is deemed paid up although continuing in force. In the UK, this is cancellation of premiums for a life assurance policy during the policy term where, instead of the policyholder applying for the cash value, he/she elects to leave premiums paid to date as a paid up policy which will give reduced benefits at maturity.

**pari passu**
Ranking equally. For example, in a new issue of shares which carry equal rights with existing shares they are said to rank pari passu.

**par value**
The issued price of a security (stocks, shares, bonds etc) which bears no relation to the market price. For example, in the UK, gilts are issued with a par value of £100 and as they are traded on the market throughout their lives their value can vary above or below £100 depending on their popularity at the time. When they reach their *redemption date* they revert to their par value of £100. Also known as nominal value/nominal price.

## partial intestacy
A situation where a *will* does not cover the whole estate of a deceased person.

## participating life insurance [USA]
*Life insurance* which pays dividends to policyholders based on the company's investment performance. The policyholder can choose whether to take the dividend in the form of cash, reinvest in the policy or pay a reduced premium.

## participating plan [UK]
A *with profits* life assurance policy which participates in the bonuses of the company.participating preference shares
[UK] *Preference shares* which, in addition to paying a specified dividend, entitles preference shareholders to participate in receiving an additional dividend if ordinary shareholders are paid a dividend above a stated amount.

## participating preferred stock [USA]
*Preferred stock* which, in addition to paying a specified dividend, entitles preferred stockholders to participate with holders of common stock in receiving any additional dividends.

## partly paid shares
In *privatisations* it is usual for shareholders to pay for their shares in two or three instalments. Until the final instalment is made the shares are only partly paid.

## partner
A person who is a member of a *partnership*.

## partnership
Two or more persons working together in the organisation and running of a business. There are two types of partners,

that is, general partners and limited partners. General partners are fully responsible for the debts of the business. Limited partners are liable only to the extent of their original investment. See also *limited liability partnership*.

**pass book**
A book of recorded transactions in a savings account, issued by banks in the US and by building societies in the UK in which a customer's deposits, withdrawals and interest are entered. The book is retained by the customer to give an indication of the running balance. See *postal account*.

**passed dividend**
The failure of a company to pay a scheduled dividend, usually because of reduced profits and often resulting in a reduction of the share price.

**pass through security [USA]**
A security backed by a pool of assets, particularly mortgages, whereby the interest and principal paid on the mortgages is passed through to the shareholder.

**pay as you earn (PAYE) [UK]**
Persons who earn income from employment or who receive a *pension* are liable for income tax under the PAYE system. Taxable pay (gross salary less pension contributions less allowances) is used by the employer to calculate a person's income tax (according to his/her notice of coding) which is passed to HM Revenue & Customs usually monthly or weekly. This ensures that employees pay their income tax on a regular basis.

**pay as you go basis [USA]**
A system of tax payment by which an employer deducts a proportion of an employee's salary for onward remittance to the Inland Revenue Service.

**PAYE emergency tax**
See *emergency tax*.

**payee**
A person to whom a payment is made.

**payer**
A person who makes a payment to a payee.

**payment card**
A plastic card, either *charge card*, *credit card* or *debit card* used by the owner to purchase goods or services or to obtain cash.

**payout ratio [USA]**
The proportion of earnings paid out in dividends to shareholders, that is, dividend payment divided by earnings.

**pecuniary legacy**
See *legacy*.

**P/E ratio**
See *price/earnings ratio*.

**penny shares [UK]**
Shares with a low value (for example 1p to 20p) traded on a stock exchange. These are often shares in small companies or those which have encountered falling profits and/or problems of debt. Relatively large quantities of shares can be purchased for modest outlays and a price movement upwards by a few pence could result in significant gains. However this type of speculation is considered to be high risk.

### penny stocks [USA]
Stocks which normally sell for $1 or less and traded in the *over the counter* market. They are highly speculative since a relatively small increase or decrease in price can result in significant gains or losses.

### Pension Benefit Guaranty Corporation (PBGC) [USA]
A federal corporation, set up in conjunction with the Employee Retirement Income Security Act (ERISA) of 1974, to guarantee basic benefits to participants in pension plans which are underfunded.

### pension forecast [UK]
Upon request, a written forecast may be obtained from the *Benefits Agency* outlining a person's estimated entitlement to the *state pension* at retirement age. It is based on certain assumptions and total NI contributions paid over the person's working life to date. The forecast takes into account the entitlements to the various segments of the state pension namely *basic pension*, *State Second Pension*, *State Earnings Related Pension Scheme* and *Graduated Pension*.

### pension fund
The total assets of a pension scheme from which a person's pension is paid.

### pension mortgage [UK]
A type of mortgage which utilises the tax free lump sum entitlement from a personal pension or stakeholder pension at retirement age to repay the *mortgage* whilst the remainder is (and must be) used to provide a *pension*. Throughout the mortgage term the borrower pays interest to the lender whilst additionally making payments into the pension scheme. Tax relief is allowable on the contributions to the pension scheme, which makes this type of plan attractive.

## pension plan/scheme

A scheme designed to provide regular payments to a person who has retired from employment. A defined benefit pension plan is one in which an employee's pension benefit is related to number of years service and final salary with each employer. A defined contributions pension plan is one in which benefits are dependent on contributions to and the growth of the pension fund.

In the USA an *individual retirement account (IRA)* is a plan which individuals may arrange for themselves. Persons who are self employed may set up a plan for themselves by way of a *Keogh pension plan*. Savings grow tax deferred until benefits are taken.

In the UK there are four main types of pension:
   State pension
   Occupationalpension
   Personal pension/stakeholder pension
   Retirement annuity contract

A person's pension, after deduction of allowances is liable for income tax.

## Pension Protection Fund [UK]

A fund established under the Pensions Act 2004 to protect members of private sector final salary pension schemes where the employer becomes insolvent with insufficient funds to maintain full scheme benefits for all members.

## Pension Schemes Office

An agency of HM Revenue & Customs, with responsibility for making sure that pension schemes comply with the tax rules and regulations governing them.

## Pension Schemes Registry [UK]

A database of all occupational and personal pension schemes and their predecessors, maintained by the Pensions

## *Pensions Advisory Service*

Regulator. It enables members who have changed jobs or lost contact with a scheme for other reasons to search for it free of charge.

### Pensions Advisory Service (TPAS) [UK]
An independent non-profit organisation that provides free information, advice and guidance about all types of pensions: state pensions, occupational schemes, personal pensions and stakeholder pensions.

### Pensions Compensation Board [UK]
Formerly an independent body set up to pay compensation to occupational pension scheme members where money had been taken dishonestly from the fund and the employer was bankrupt. Its function was taken over by the *Pension Protection Fund*.

### Pensions Ombudsman [UK]
An independent body established by the Social Security Act 1990 to deal with complaints about the administration of occupational pension schemes. It is not part of the *Financial Ombudsman Service*.

### Pensions Regulator [UK]
The regulatory body for UK occupational pension schemes. Its objectives are to protect scheme members' benefits, to promote good administration, and to reduce the likelihood of compensation claims on the *Pension Protection Fund*.

### peppercorn rent
A nominal rent intended to demonstrate that a property is *leasehold* and not *freehold*.

## *permanent interest bearing shares*

**performance bond**
A form of guarantee, given by the seller in a contract, that in the event of the terms of the contract not being fulfilled, the buyer will be able to claim compensation in the form of money.

**performance fund [USA]**
A *mutual fund* with an objective of capital growth with little or no dividend payments.

**performance stock [USA]**
A stock whose price is anticipated to grow at an above average rate but with little or no dividend payments.

**periodic payment plan [USA]**
A plan to build up capital in a *mutual fund* by regular investments, typically on a monthly or quarterly basis.

**permanent health insurance [UK]**
In return for regular premiums, PHI provides an income in the event of the policy holder being unable to work due to illness or injury. There is no payment on death. Benefits are paid usually after a waiting period of several months or even a year known as the *deferment period* and usually continue to retirement age. During the deferment period the employer will often pay the employee's salary. The benefit payable will normally be no greater than 65% of earnings in the year preceding the disability less the amount of the state incapacity benefit. This is to encourage persons to return to work in the event of partial or full recovery. If a claim becomes payable, the policyholder will receive payment free of tax.

**permanent interest bearing shares (PIBS) [UK]**
*Fixed interest securities* where the rate of interest is known as the *coupon*. They are issued by building societies to enable them to raise capital and are tradable on the Stock Exchange.

### perpetual bond

The yield is relatively high but there is no *redemption date*. This means that the original investment can only be recouped by selling on the open market which is rather small and therefore PIBS may be difficult to sell. Any profit which is made on a sale is not subject to *capital gains tax* although the interest payments are liable to *income tax*.

### perpetual bond
A bond without a maturity date which pays interest indefinitely.

### perquisite (perk)
A benefit given to an employee in addition to his/her salary such as a company car, pension contributions and free products.

### personal accident insurance
An insurance policy which, in return for regular premiums, pays a specific sum in the event of death, loss of sight or limbs or other permanent disablement due to an accident.

### personal accident and sickness insurance
An insurance policy similar to *personal accident insurance* with the additional benefit of cover against disablement due to sickness.

### personal accounts
A company's sales accounts of customers contained in the sales *ledger* and purchase accounts of suppliers contained in the purchase ledger are also known as personal accounts. See *ledger*.

### personal allowance [UK]
An allowance, granted to all UK residents, which is deductible from *gross income*, which together with any other allowances reduce a person's *taxable pay*.

### personal equity plan (PEP) [UK]
Formerly a plan where persons over the age of 18 could invest in shares and qualifying *unit trusts* and *investment trusts* in a tax-efficient way. New PEPs were discontinued in 1999 and replaced by *individual savings accounts* (ISAs). Finally, any remaining PEPs were converted into ISAs in 2008.

### personal exemption [USA]
The amount a person may subtract from *personal income* when computing federal and state income tax

### personal identification number (PIN)
A set of numbers (usually four) which the owner of a *payment card* uses when making purchases or withdrawing cash from an automated teller machine (cash dispenser).

### personal income [USA]
A person's total income which includes salary, *transfer payments*, dividend and interest income etc.

### Personal Investment Authority (PIA) [UK]
Formerly a *Self Regulating Organisation (SRO)* that supervised companies conducting investment business with private investors in the financial services market. Now superseded by the *Financial Services Authority*.

### personal ledger
A book in which the *personal accounts* of a company are kept that is, the sales ledger and the purchase ledger. See *ledger*.

### personal loan
Loans available from banks and other financial institutions to private individuals for personal use such as the purchase of

a motor vehicle, holiday or similar item. Repayment periods vary typically from one year to five years.

### personal pension plan [UK]
A savings scheme with taxation advantages introduced by the government during the latter part of the 1980s to enable the self employed to build up a pension fund for retirement. Since *A-Day* it is available also to all employees and even (up to contributions of £3,600 p.a.) to persons with no earned income. The PPP is a *money purchase scheme* and effectively replaced what was known as a *retirement annuity contract (RAC)*, also known as a Section 226 policy, which, unless in force before 30th June1988 is no longer available. Contributions to PPPs receive full tax relief up to maximum permitted HM Revenue & Customs limits. An employer may contribute to an employee's PPP but this is not obligatory. Also a PPP may be used to contract out of *S2P*.

As with all pension funds, capital gains within the fund are free of tax. Retirement can be taken between the ages of 50 (55 from 2010) and 75 although it is not necessary to stop working. At retirement up to 25% of the pension fund can be taken as a tax free lump sum with the balance being used to purchase an *annuity* (the pension). Alternatively, the buying of an annuity with the fund balance can be deferred whilst drawing an 'income' from it;broadly speaking this income cannot exceed an amount equivalent to what would have been received from an annuity. See also *stakeholder pension*.

### personal possessions
The personal possessions of a deceased person which pass to the *beneficiary* or beneficiaries of the *residue of estate* unless otherwise stated in the *will*.

## *polarisation*

**petty cash**
Cash held by a company on its premises to cover small items of expense. A record of such transactions is usually kept in a petty cash book.

**phased retirement [UK]**
The arrangement of a *personal pension plan* in segments to enable the policy holder to take a pension in stages. The lump sum entitlement is also phased. The policy holder may elect to phase the purchase of an annuity or to phase income drawdown (see personal pension plan).

**physicals**
See *actuals*.

**physical delivery**
The settlement of a *futures* contract by receipt or delivery of a *commodity*

**PIN number**
See *personal identification number*.

**pit**
An area within a *futures* exchange where trading in a particular futures or *options contract* is conducted by *open outcry*.

**place (placing)**
The sale of a company's shares to chosen institutions. This can enable a company to join the stockmarket or raise further capital for a *listed company*.

**polarisation [UK]**
Although the term polarisation is no longer officially used, financial advisers are still required to inform their clients of their status under the terms of the Financial Services and Markets Act 2000, i.e. whether they offer advice on products

from the whole market, or from a limited range of specified providers, or from a single provider.

### policy document
The document which forms the contract between the insured, that is, the person taking out insurance and the insurer (the insurance company).

### policy loan [USA]
The amount a life insurance policyholder may borrow against the *cash surrender value*. Interest is payable on the loan which may be deducted from the cash surrender value. In the event of the death of the policyholder any loan outstanding plus interest is deductible from the death benefit.
[UK] A loan granted by a life assurance company to a policyholder. The extent of the loan is based on a percentage of the surrender value (typically up to 90%) of a *whole life* or *endowment policy*.

### poll tax
See *community charge*.

### Ponzi scheme
A fraudulent pyramid-type investment scheme in which the returns to existing investors are paid out from the receipt of new capital from new investors.

### portability [USA]
The capability of a pension plan holder to transfer pension benefits when changing employment.

### portfolio
A schedule of the investments of an institution or individual. In the case of an institution, such as a *mutual fund* or *unit trust*, investing for say capital growth, details would typically list the range of companies and the holding in each as a

percentage of the trust total. For an individual, the portfolio would typically list holdings in equities, bonds, mutual funds, unit trusts, investment trusts and bank deposits etc.

**postal account**
In the UK, a *bank* or *building society* account in which all transactions are conducted via post. Though still available, they are increasingly being replaced by accounts operated over the internet or by telephone.

**Post Office Savings**
See *National Savings & Investments*.

**postdated check (cheque)**
A check with a future date entered. Funds cannot be transferred until that date is reached.

**posting**
The recording of an entry in a ledger

**potentially exempt transfer (PET) [UK]**
A gift from one person to another person or body which is not liable to inheritance tax provided the person making the gift lives for at least seven years after the transfer is made. Should death occur before seven years tax will become payable, the amount being related to the number of years following the transfer prior to death according to the table below.

| Time from transfer of gift to death | Percentage of inheritance tax payable |
|---|---|
| up to 3 years | 100% |
| 3 to 4 years | 80% |
| 4 to 5 years | 60% |
| 5 to 6 years | 40% |
| 6 to 7 years | 20% |

Any tax which becomes payable is normally charged to the recipient of the gift but in certain circumstances the liability may revert to the donor.

### pound cost averaging
In the UK, the regular investing of fixed amounts over regular periods, typically monthly, in order to accumulate holdings in securities such as shares, unit trusts and investment trusts. When for example a unit trust price or investment trust price has fallen then more units or shares will be purchased for that month. Similarly when the price rises then fewer units or shares will be purchased. Over a period of a few years, the average price paid will be lower than the average share price for that period since more shares are bought at the lower price and fewer at the higher price. Similar to dollar cost averaging or constant dollar plan in the USA.

### power of attorney
A document which authorises a person to act on behalf of another.

### pre-tax profit
See *profit before tax*.

### precious metals
The metals gold, silver and platinum. In the UK, gold and silver are traded on the *London Bullion Market*.

### preference shares [UK]
The shares of a company, which pay a fixed dividend and which may have a *redemption date* (the date when the original investment is repaid) at a fixed or variable time in the future. They carry no voting rights unless dividends are in arrears. *Ordinary shares* carry voting rights and pay dividends in relation to the company's profits which could be generous when profits are high but poor or even non-

existent in bad times. Preference shares receive dividends before ordinary shares and in the event of the winding up of a company rank higher for repayment.

### preferential form
Companies listed on the *London Stock Exchange* offering shares to the public are allowed to set aside up to 10% of the issue for application from employees and from shareholders of a parent company floating a subsidiary via a preferential form.

### preferred stock [USA]
Stock which pays a fixed dividend and which carries preference over common stock both for dividend payment and claim on assets in the event of liquidation. This type of stock does not normally carry voting rights. Most preferred stock is cumulative (*cumulative preferred stock*) which means that in the event of a dividend being passed, that is, not paid, it accumulates and must subsequently be paid before the dividends of common stock.

### premium
1. A lump sum or regular payment in return for a contract of *insurance*
2. When the market price of a *new issue* of shares is higher than the *issue price* the difference is known as the premium.
3. When the share price of an *investment trust* is higher than its *net asset value* per share, the shares are said to trade at a premium.
4. The purchase price of an *option*.
5. The amount paid by an investor over the current share price by purchasing shares via the *warrants*. This is the amount by which the *exercise price(2)* plus the warrant price exceeds the share price

## premium bonds
See *National Savings and Investments*.

## prepayment fee
In the US, a fee charged to a borrower by a lender when a loan or mortgage is repaid ahead of schedule. In the UK, lenders may impose a similar charge, often called an early repayment fee.

## price
The cost of purchasing a security (shares, bonds etc.).

## price earnings ratio (P/E ratio)
A company's share price divided by its *earnings per share*.
    For example: Share price = $15
    Earnings per Share = $1.50
    Price Earnings ratio = $15/$1.50 = 10
A company's P/E ratio shows how high its shares are priced in relation to its earnings. It can also be used as a guide to compare with other companies in the same *sector*. If the sector average is say 14 and the company in question has a P/E ratio of 10, it could be seen as being relatively sluggish in growth prospects. If another company in the same sector has a P/E ratio of 18 it could indicate a growth company and thus its shares are in demand, so pushing up the share price.

## primary market
A market in which *new issues* are traded. A secondary market is a market in which trading of existing securities takes place.

## prime rate [USA]
The interest rate which banks offer to their prime customers, that is, those with the most creditworthy records. The UK equivalent is *base rate*.

## principal
1. A person or company for whom an *agent* acts.
2. The *face value* of a debt instrument such as a bond or a note.

## prior charges
The fixed liabilities of an *investment trust* including *loan capital* and usually *preference shares*. The subtraction of these charges from total assets gives the *net asset value* of the trust. Prior charges may be expressed either at *par value* or current *market value*.

## prior preferred stock [USA]
Preferred stock with priority over other issues of preferred stock for the payment of dividends and in the event of liquidation.

## private company [UK]
A company which is not a *public limited company (plc)*. It may be a *limited company* or unlimited. Private limited companies may not offer shares to the public but may do so to their staff.

## private equity
Medium-term or long-term finance offered in exchange for a shareholding in a private limited company. Capital for private equity is channelled through private equity companies and is raised mainly from financial institutions or wealthy individuals.

## private medical insurance
An insurance policy which provides cover in respect of the cost of private medical treatment. This typically includes such items as the fees of consultants, surgeons and anaesthetists, costs of operating theatres and hospital rooms, X-rays, radiotherapy, chemotherapy, drugs and dressings etc.

### privatisation
The transferring of ownership of publicly owned or nationalised companies (that is, state controlled companies) to the private sector. This is accomplished via an *offer for sale*.

### pro forma invoice
An invoice presented by one company to another for payment for goods prior to their despatch. This method of invoicing is to ensure payment is received and is often the case when two companies have not traded before. If future trading is anticipated it will then be usual for an account to be set up for the purchasing company with credit facilities.

### probate
The legal procedure by which a will is authenticated and which confirms the authority of the executors to administer its contents.

### profit and loss statement (P&L)
A set of accounts, usually prepared annually, which depict a company's trading performance and normally read in conjunction with the *balance sheet* and *cash flow* data. The profit and loss account can broadly be shown as follows:
Turnover (sales) less manufacturing costs (or cost of sales if for example a retailing company) = gross profit or loss
Gross profit plus any non trading income (for example sale of vehicles) less *operating costs* = operating profit
Operating profit less interest payments to banks or loan stock = net profit before tax (pre tax profit)
Net profit less tax = net profit after tax
Part of the net profit after tax may be used to pay a *dividend* with the balance being retained within the business for future investment.

## profit before tax
A company's net profit before deduction of *corporation tax*.

## profit sharing scheme
A scheme where part of a company's profits are paid to employees as an incentive for loyalty and application to the job. The reward may be given via cash, shares or a combination of both.

## profit taking
The selling of *securities* (for example, shares) when the price has risen in order to lock in to profits.

## promissory note
A signed statement promising to pay to a specified person or the bearer a particular sum of money on a fixed date or on demand.

## proof of title
In the UK, when a claimant makes a claim in respect of *life assurance*, he/she will have to provide evidence of identity and that he/she is entitled to the proceeds, invariably by submitting the policy document. In the event of a claim following the death of the *life assured*, the death certificate will also need to be submitted to the insurers by the legal representatives of the deceased.

## property
An item which is owned, for example a motor car, furniture, paintings, tools etc. These are known as personal property. Buildings and land are known as real property. See *property bond*.

## property bond
A bond issued by *life insurance* companies to investors whose premiums are invested in property.

## property income taxation
See *income from property*.

## property tax [USA]
A tax charged on real property and assessed by consideration to its use. For example whether the land is used for residential, commercial or industrial purposes. In the UK a form of property tax is the *council tax*.

## proposal form
A form which is completed by a person applying for a life policy and which forms the basis of the contract.

## ProShare [UK]
A not-for-profit organisation, part of the ifs School of Finance, that represents the Employee Share Ownership industry to the media, governments and regulatory and statutory bodies.

## prospect
A person who is not currently a client or customer who may (or may not) purchase a product from the seller. If such a person subsequently does buy, he/she becomes a client.

## prospectus
A document which sets out a company's financial history, performance, *capital structure* and future prospects, when shares or other securities are offered for sale to the public.

## protected rights [UK]
Pension benefits derived from funds built up from minimum contributions paid into an *appropriate personal pension plan* by the *Department for Work and Pensions*. These benefits are a substitute for part of the additional state pension (e.g. S2P).

**proxy**
A person who acts on behalf of a member of a company for the purpose of voting at a company meeting.

**prudential supervision [UK]**
A term sometimes used to describe the supervision/regulation of institutions such as banks and insurance companies, where the supervising authority (the FSA) seeks to ensure that the protection of depositors, borrowers and other customers is maintained by the institution in question being financially sound.

**public limited company (plc)**
A company registered as a public company and which must display the letters plc after its name. Its shares may be offered to the public.

**public offering**
An offering of new securities to the public. Sometimes known as public issue.

**Public Sector Borrowing Requirement (PSBR)**
See *Public Sector Net Cash Requirement (PSNCR)*.

**Public Sector Net Cash Requirement (PSNCR) [UK]**
Formerly known as Public Sector Borrowing Requirement (PSBR), PSNCR is the difference between the expenditure of the public sector and its income. Where there is a deficit it is financed by borrowing, that is, principally via the sale of government gilt edged stocks (gilts). Public sector net borrowing also measures the difference between the expenditure and income of the public sector but differs from the net cash requirement in that it is measured on an accruals basis whereas the net cash requirement is mainly a cash measure.

**purchased life annuity**
See *annuity*.

**purchase ledger**
See *ledger*.

**purchasing power [USA]**
The amount of goods and services which can be purchased by a dollar after taking into account the effect of inflation. Purchasing power can be assessed by tracking an index of consumer prices and comparing different periods, for example the early 1990s and the current time. Inflation will result in reduced purchasing power over a period of time.

**pure endowment [UK]**
A *life assurance* policy where the *sum assured* is paid if the *life assured* survives the term but in the event of prior death nothing is payable.

**put option**
An *option* which gives the *holder* the right but not the obligation to sell a stated quantity of the *underlying instrument* (for example, shares, indices, commodities, etc.) at a specified price on or before a given date.

### qualification period [USA]
That period of time, as stated in an insurance policy, during which benefits are not payable to the insured following a claim. This period is to enable the insurance company to confirm that the claim is genuine and is usual in health insurance.

### qualified plan [USA]
A *tax deferred* pension plan set up by an employer to enable employees to accumulate tax free savings for retirement benefits. Usually, contributions are made by employer and employee and when income is taken at retirement it is taxable.

### qualified stock option [USA]
A *stock option*, given to executives and employees, which complies with the requirements of the Internal Revenue Service. A qualified stock option is not subject to tax at the grant date or when exercised.

### qualifying annuity [USA]
An *annuity* which is purchased within a *qualified plan*.

### qualifying policy [UK]
The proceeds from a *life assurance* policy to an individual are free of tax provided the policy is qualifying. Additionally, if the policy was in force before 14th March 1984, tax relief can be claimed on the premiums (known as *life assurance premium relief*). The rules which govern qualification are:

a) The premiums must be payable for ten years or 75% of the term whichever is the shorter.
b) The premiums must be paid regularly on an annual or more frequent basis such as monthly.
c) The sum assured must be at least 75% of the total premiums payable over the life of the policy.

## quantitative easing

The creation of a specified quantity of new money through the open market operations of a Central Bank. The purpose is to kick-start an increase the money supply as a first step in moving an economy out of recession.

## quartile

*Unit trusts* or *investment trusts* within given *sectors* may be ranked to compare their performance. Each sector is divided into four groups by descending order of performance with each group being known respectively as 1st, 2nd, 3rd and 4th quartiles. For example if a sector contains thirty six trusts, each quartile will contain nine trusts. Trusts will often advertise their performance over various periods (for example, one, three, five and ten years) by indicating, say, a first quartile ranking which in the above case would indicate a position in the top nine.

## quotation

On a stock market the highest bid price and the lowest offer price of a security available at a particular time.

## quoted company

See *listed company*.

## quoted price

The price of a *security* or *commodity*.

# R

### raider
An individual or organisation who seeks to take over a company by purchasing its shares.

### random walk
The theory that share price movements are not linked in any way to their past history. This is in complete contrast to charting where *chartists* predict future trends based on past movement.

### rating [USA]
The classification of the quality of bonds by various rating services. A bond with the highest rating is classified as AAA. See *bond rating*.

### real account
A *ledger* account detailing assets and capital (such as buildings and machinery).

### real estate
Property comprising land and buildings, fences etc as opposed to personal property. Also known as real property.

### real estate agent [USA]
An agent engaged by a real estate broker.

### real estate broker [USA]
One who arranges the sale and purchase of property in return for a commission. Known as an estate agent in the UK.

### real estate investment trust (REIT)
A publicly traded investment trust which invests the capital of its shareholders in a variety of real estate.

### real property
See *real estate*.

### real time
A reference made to actual time in a computer process. For example a company selling a product in varying volume and using a computer real time process would be able to establish from any of its terminals the balance of stock immediately after any sales through any of those terminals.

### receiver
A person appointed by a court to wind up the affairs of a company and to utilise assets to pay its *creditors*.

### recession
A decrease in *gross national product (GNP)* for two consecutive quarters. A severe recession is known as a *depression* or slump.

### Recognised Clearing House [UK]
An organisation authorised by the *Financial Services Authority (FSA)* to provide facilities to clear and settle UK trades.

### Recognised Investment Exchange [UK]
An *investment* exchange which meets the requirements for recognition under the *Financial Services and Markets Act 2000* and is approved by the *Financial Services Authority (FSA)* to provide markets for investments.

## Recognised Professional Body (RPB) [UK]
A body which regulates the practice of a profession such as the Institute of Chartered Accountants, The Law Society and the Institute of Actuaries. RPBs no longer regulate the financial services activities of their members; many solicitors (for example) have separate financial advice organisations that are directly authorised and regulated by the *Financial Services Authority*.

## recovery stocks/shares
Shares which have decreased in value but are considered to be capable of recovering to their former price.

## redeemable
Something which can be bought back by the original issuer from the purchaser.

## redeemable preference shares
*Preference shares* which the issuing company reserves the right to redeem. The shares may or may not have a specific *redemption date* or dates.

## redemption
The re-purchase of a *debt security* such as a bond, or *preferred stock* by the issuing company at or before maturity.

## redemption date
The actual date on which repayment of a *bond* or *loan stock* takes place.

## redemption fees [USA]
Fees imposed by a *mutual fund* on shareholders who dispose of shares within a relatively short period after purchase.

**redemption price [USA]**
The price at which a *bond* or *preferred stock* can be redeemed by the issuer.

**redemption yield**
See *yield*.

**refer to drawer**
A phrase used by banks in the UK when a cheque is dishonoured or 'bounced'.

**registered securities**
Shares and bonds etc where holders have their names kept in a register maintained by the issuing company.

**registrar**
1. A person with responsibility for keeping a register of records and transactions.
2. An organisation with responsibility for keeping a register of bonds and stock issues.

**Registrar of Companies**
The chief executive of *Companies House*, the official body with responsibility for the registration of all companies in the UK.

**reimbursement**
The repayment of a person who has incurred expenses on behalf of another. For example the reimbursement of an employee who has paid money on business related expenses (such as travel expenses) on behalf of his/her employer.

**reinsurance**
The covering of all or some of an insurance risk by an insurer by transferring to another insurer in return for the payment or part payment of premiums.

### reinvestment of dividends
Instead of a cash dividend being paid to a shareholder, the dividend amount is used to purchase more shares.

### remortgage
The arranging of alternative finance for the purchase of a property which is already mortgaged. For example obtaining a mortgage with a lower interest rate to replace the existing mortgage.

### renewable term life insurance [USA] renewable term assurance [UK]
Term life insurance with a term for example of three years, at the end of which the policy can be renewed for a further three years and similarly thereafter for an overall specified length of time.

### renounceable documents
Documents which provide temporary evidence of ownership of unregistered shares. These include a company's offer of shares to the public, a *rights issue* and a capitalisation or *scrip issue*. In each case instructions are given regarding action to be taken if the holder requires to have the shares registered in his/her name or if it is required to renounce them in favour of another person.

### rent
Regular payment by a *tenant* to an owner for the use of his/her land or buildings.

### renunciation
The relinquishing of shares by one person to another by the completion of a renunciation form usually attached to the *allotment letter*.

### repayment mortgage
A *mortgage* where throughout the *term*, regular payments (usually monthly) are made to partly repay interest on the capital and to partly repay the capital itself (the amount of the loan). Initially the large proportion of the repayments will be used to pay interest since the capital amount outstanding is at its highest value. Therefore over the initial years the capital will not reduce very much. However as the years proceed more and more of the monthly repayments will be applied to reducing the capital until towards the end of the term the large proportion will be paying off capital and a small proportion paying interest. In the event that interest rates rise then often the monthly repayments will rise accordingly. Alternatively to keep the same monthly repayments the term will need to be extended. If interest rates fall then the reverse applies. It is usually a wise precaution, and may be a requirement of the lender, that the borrower takes out *life assurance* so that repayment is made in the event of his/her death during the term.

### repo rate
The interest rate implied by transactions between a central bank and retail banks by means of which the central bank maintains liquidity in the banking system. The Bank of England's repo rate is often known as its base rate.

### reserves
Mainly the retained profits of a company and forming part of its *capital*.

### residence and domicile [UK]
A person's residence or domicile status can determine their liability to UK income tax, capital gains tax and inheritance tax. Tax rules are immensely complicated, but broadly speaking:

### 1) Resident in the UK
Residence relates mainly to income tax and capital gains tax. A person who is present in the UK for at least 183 days in a tax year is treated as resident and is normally subject to UK income and capital gains taxes. Double taxation agreements are in place with many countries to avoid income or gains being taxed twice.

### 2) Domiciled in the UK
Domicile of origin is the domicile of your father at the date of your birth (not the place of your birth). This can be changed to domicile of choice by moving to another country with the intention of remaining there permanently. Domicile relates mainly to inheritance tax (IHT): for UK-domiciled persons, IHT is due on the transfer of property located anywhere in the world, but for non-UK-domiciled persons it applies only to property located in the UK.

**residuary estate**
The remainder of an estate after the payment of debts, expenses and taxes and the distribution of *legacies*. Also known as residue of estate in the UK.

**residuary legacy**
See *legacy*.

**resistance level**
Price levels at which shares stop rising. See *support level*.

**retail investor**
US term for an investor who buys securities on his/her behalf through a stockbroker.

**retail price index (RPI)**
An index of the prices of goods in retail outlets used to measure the rate of *inflation*.

### retailer card
A plastic *payment card* issued by a specific retailer or group of retailers for limited use at their own outlets. Normally known as a store card in the UK.

### retained earnings
That proportion of a company's profits after tax, not paid in dividends but reinvested in the *capital* of the company.

### retirement
The termination of employment at which time salary/wages/earnings are replaced by a pension.

### retirement annuity contract [UK]
Prior to 30th June 1988, persons not in pensionable employment (employment where no pension scheme exists) or persons who were self employed were able to qualify for tax relief for contributions made to a pension scheme known as a retirement annuity under section 226 of the Income and Corporation Taxes Act 1970. Although RACs were replaced by *personal pension plans* from 1st July 1988 those already in force may continue to operate.

### retirement pension forecast
See *pension forecast*.

### return on investment
The overall profit (or loss) expressed as a percentage of the original investment. For example: A person invests $5,000 in the shares of a company and some time later has received £100 in dividends with the value of the shares now $5,200. Return on investment will be:

$[(\$100 + \$5,200 - \$5,000)/\$5,000] \times 100 = (\$300/\$5,000) \times 100 = 6\%$.

### revenue account
An *investment trust* term referring to analysis of investment income. This details whether income is *franked* or unfranked and whether the source of income is from UK investments, overseas or unlisted securities.

### reverse annuity mortgage (RAM) [USA]
A mortgage that permits a normally elderly person or persons who own their home outright to receive an income for life in return for gradually relinquishing ownership in the property.

### reverse mortgage [USA]
A mortgage that permits a normally elderly person or persons who own their home outright to receive an income with the home as collateral. The loan is repaid plus interest either at the end of the term or on the death of the borrower when the property would be sold.

### reverse leverage [USA]
The investment of borrowed money where the return fails to match the interest payable on the loan.

### reversionary bonus [UK]
A bonus added to the *sum assured* (or *basic sum assured*) of a *with profits* life assurance policy out of a life company's surplus profits usually on an annual basis. These bonuses are payable at the end of the *term* of the policy (that is, at *maturity*) or on prior death of the *life assured* and once allocated, their values are guaranteed provided premiums are paid up to maturity or death. The values of such bonuses are usually related to the sum assured and can be either simple reversionary bonuses (related to the sum assured only) or compound reversionary bonuses (related to the sum assured plus bonuses to date). Reversionary bonuses may sometimes

### right of redemption

be taken in cash at the time they are declared but the values will be significantly lower compared with leaving them until maturity. See *terminal bonus*.

### right of redemption [USA]
The right to recover property forfeited by *foreclosure* by paying the outstanding principal owed plus interest. Known in the UK as equity of redemption.

### right of survivorship
The right of a joint owner to full title of a property when the death of the other joint owner occurs.

### rights issue
An invitation by a *listed firm* or *listed company* to its shareholders to purchase additional shares to enable it to raise new capital. The offer is usually to purchase a quantity of new shares in proportion to those already owned and at a discount to the current market price. For example in a one for five rights issue, a shareholder would be invited to buy one new share for every five shares owned. The discount could typically be around 20%. Also known, particularly in the USA, as a rights offering.

### rights offering
See *rights issue*.

### risk/reward
A broad general rule of investment states: the greater the risk, the greater the potential for higher rewards. For example a *capital* sum deposited with a bank or building society will usually be very safe since it is rare for either to fail, and in many cases a compensation scheme is available. The capital, whilst remaining relatively safe will also earn interest. However such interest will be partially devalued by

*inflation* and will not normally be particularly competitive over the long term. On the other hand investment in equities (shares, mutual funds, unit trusts, investment trusts etc) will normally over the long term give greater returns but the risk is much higher. Also in the short term they could easily fall in value. Investors therefore usually seek to build a balanced *portfolio* of investments to include low risk deposits for safety (bank deposits, bonds) and longer term higher risk instruments such as equities for greater potential growth.

**risk capital**
See *venture capital*.

**rolling settlement [UK]**
Prior to 1994, purchases and sales of *securities* were combined during an *account* period (normally ten working days) and the net amount settled on the second Monday following that account period. Now a rolling settlement basis is used with settlement of all deals due five days after dealing.
The purpose of this and other changes was to reduce the settlement periods and generally speed up transactions. See *CREST*.

**rollover**
1. The transferring of funds from one investment to another such as rolling over the proceeds from a bond which has matured into another bond.
2. The term used when a borrower obtains authority from a bank to delay a principal payment on a loan.
3. The movement of a *futures* or *options* position from one delivery/expiry month to a further dated month by trading out of the existing position and simultaneously trading into the further dated month.

### rollover relief [UK]
A capital gain on the disposal of certain businesses and business assets can be deferred ('rolled over' to a new business) if the proceeds of the disposal are reinvested in another business / other assets. This must take place between one year before and three years after the disposal.

### round lot [USA]
The normal *trading unit* on a securities exchange. A round lot on the New York Stock Exchange is 100 for shares and $1,000 face value for a bond.

### round trip
The opening purchase or sale of a *futures* or *options contract* and the subsequent opposite and closing sale or purchase in the same contract. It is usual for transaction costs to be quoted on a round trip basis.

### round-trip trading
A market manipulation practice used to artificially inflate the apparent volume of (and revenue from) transactions by continually selling, repurchasing and re-selling assets such as commodities or securities.

### Royal Mint [UK]
The organisation responsible to the Chancellor of the Exchequer for the manufacture of coins. Banknotes are the responsibility of the Bank of England.

### rule of 72
An approximation used to roughly estimate the number of years required for an investment to double in value at a given rate of compound interest. The number 72 is divided by the compound interest rate to find the period required.

**The International Dictionary of Personal Finance**

### S2P [UK]
The state second pension, the current (since 2002) version of the additional state pension, available only to employed persons, who are obliged to be in S2P unless are contracted out by their employer's scheme or contract themselves out using an *appropriate personal pension*.

### salary reduction plan [USA]
A *tax deferred* retirement plan which provides for an employee to have a certain amount of gross salary withheld and invested in a choice of stocks and bonds. Contributions and fund growth are free of tax until withdrawal.

### sales ledger
See *ledger*.

### sales charge
A brokerage fee charged to a buyer of shares in a *mutual fund*. The charge is deducted prior to the balance being invested in the fund.

### sales tax [USA]
A state or local government tax levied on goods and services. The amount of tax is based on a percentage of the selling price. An item costing $100 and a sales tax of 5% will cost in total $105.

### save as you earn (SAYE) [UK]
A tax-efficient 3-year or 5-year savings scheme designed to encourage employees to save towards buying shares in the

company they work for. At the end of the term, savers can use their fund to buy shares at a price set at the beginning of the scheme. Alternatively they can take the cash.

## savings account

An account with a bank or financial institution where savings are made. Interest is paid usually once or twice per year and will be relative to the amount of money in the account and current interest rates. There is often a notice period required for withdrawals and the longer this term the higher the interest rate. In the USA savings accounts are insured up to $100,000 at banks insured by the Federal Deposit Insurance Corporation. In the UK, compensation up to a maximum of £50,000 is payable where an authorised bank or building society fails. See *Financial Services Compensation Scheme*.

## savings and loan association [USA]

A financial institution in which depositors' savings are used to provide home mortgages loans. Also known a thrift institution. Broadly equivalent to a building society in the UK.

## savings element [USA]

The cash value which accumulates within a life insurance policy. The premium is applied to give both life cover plus a savings element which is allowed to grow tax deferred until withdrawn.

## schedule

That part of an *insurance* or *assurance* policy which sets out the particular details relevant to a contract. Details which are listed are typically the policy name and number, the policyholder's name, the commencement and maturity dates, the benefits payable, the life or lives assured in the case of life assurance and the premiums payable etc.

## Schedule A, B, C, D, E, F
Formerly the subdivisions of forms of income for UK income tax purposes. No longer used.

## scrip dividend [UK]
The issue of additional shares by a company to a shareholder equivalent to the cash value of the dividend if he/she chooses this method of payment.

## scrip issue
The issuing of additional shares by a company to its shareholders in proportion to their existing holdings but resulting in a correspondingly lower market price. This is achieved by the company by transferring funds from reserves into capital. For example: A person owns 1000 shares with a current price of £6 per share. If the company makes a 2 for 1 scrip issue (that is, for every share owned two further shares will be issued) the shareholder will now own 3000 shares but the price will adjust to £2 per share and the overall value will remain at £6000. The main purpose of this exercise is to make the shares more marketable in that there will be a lot more in circulation and the price more attractive at the lower level.

## SEAQ International
The London Stock Exchange's electronic price quotation system for non UK securities.

## seasoned issue
A security issued by a well established and sound performing company with generally high *liquidity*.

## seat
A membership on a securities or commodities exchange.

## second hand endowment
See *traded endowment policy*.

## second mortgage
The taking out of a *mortgage* on a property which is already mortgaged. This can be used to raise capital if the property has significantly increased in value; second mortgages are available from banks, building societies and finance companies. Since the first mortagee (lender) usually holds the deeds of the property, the second mortgagee will carry a higher risk and thus charges a considerably higher rate of interest.

## secondary market
A market in which trading of existing securities takes place. (for example on a stock exchange). Also traded on a stock exchange are *new issues* that is, a *primary market*.

## Section 32 buyout bond [UK]
Section 32 of the Finance Act 1981 allows a person to transfer a payment representing the value of pension benefits from a previous employer (that is, from an *occupational pension scheme*) to a pension plan operated by an insurance company. Single premium products used for this purpose are known as Section 32 buyout bonds.

## Section 226 policy
See *retirement annuity contract (RAC)*.

## Section 352 of the Income and Corporation Taxes Act 1988
See *certificate of deduction of tax*.

## sector
A group of companies with similar products or services which is listed with financial information such as share prices and yield etc. This information is published in the national press.

## Securities and Investments Board

For example reference to the chemicals sector in a financial newspaper enables share price performance of companies engaged in chemical products and services to be compared.

**sector fund**
A *mutual fund* or *unit trust* which invests in a specific *sector* such as chemicals or telecommunications.

**secured bond**
A bond which is secured by the guarantee of assets or collateral.

**secured loan**
A loan where the borrower offers an asset to which the lender has access in the event of the borrower failing to make the loan repayments.

**secured creditor**
A *creditor* who has a charge over the assets of a *debtor* in the event of the debtor failing to meet his/her obligations.

### Securities and Exchange Commission (SEC) [USA]
A federal agency with primary responsibility for regulating US financial markets in order to protect investors against fraudulent dealings by way of full public *disclosure*. It regulates the securities industry, stock exchanges and options markets, including electronic securities markets.

### Securities and Futures Authority (SFA) [UK]
Formerly the body regulating stockbrokers and other firms in the securities and derivatives markets. Now replaced by the *Financial Services Authority*.

### Securities and Investments Board (SIB) [UK]
Formerly the body with overall responsibility (reporting to the Chancellor of the Exchequer) for the regulation of the

## Securities Investor Protection Corporation

UK investment market in accordance with the Financial Services Act 1986. It was replaced by the *Financial Services Authority (FSA)* in October 1997.

### Securities Investor Protection Corporation (SIPC) [USA]

A non profit organization which provides insurance for cash and securities in customer accounts held by approved brokerage firms. Brokers and dealers registered with the *Securities and Exchange Commission* are obliged to be members of SIPC. In the event that such a firm fails, investors are covered up to a maximum of $500,000 of which no more than $100,000 can be cash.

### security

1. A financial asset such as a share or bond.
2. An asset which is offered by a borrower to a lender to safeguard a loan.

### segmentation

A number of small identical policies (for example, life insurance or pension policies) rather than a single large policy. Use of this arrangement can be helpful when taking a pension in that it allows *phased retirement* according to the requirements of the policyholder.

### Self Assessment [UK]

From April 1996 all taxpayers in the UK were obliged by law to maintain records of their income of all types and capital gains so as to enable tax returns to be completed. This is known as Self Assessment. Those people who normally complete a tax return must do so together with one or more schedules, the latter being relevant to the individual's particular circumstances – for example employees must complete the schedule for employment income. Upon completion of the returns and schedules, individuals may themselves calculate the tax due or submit them to *HM Revenue & Customs* to make the calculations. Alternatively the services and advice of an accountant can be obtained.

**Self Regulating Organisations (SROs) [UK]**
Formerly the three bodies set up to regulate companies dealing in investment business, with the objective of investor protection. They were the *Securities and Futures Authority (SFA)*, the *Personal Investment Authority (PIA)* and the *Investment Management Regulatory Organisation (IMRO)*. Their responsibilities are now carried out by the *Financial Services Authority*.

**senior debt [USA]**
A debt which receives priority for repayment in the event of a corporation's liquidation.

**senior mortgage bond [USA]**
A mortgage bond which receives priority on the assets of a company over other bonds in the event of liquidation.

**serial bond**
A bond which is arranged to be repaid in instalments over a period of time.

**series**
*Options contracts* on the same instrument (for example an index such as the FT-SE 100 Index) having the same *exercise price* and *expiry date* are known as the same series. *Put options* and *call options* having the same exercise price and expiry date are two different series.

**settlement**
1. The payment of monies owed following dealing on a stock exchange. Currently the period allowed is three days after the trade in the US and five days in the UK. See *rolling settlement*.

**settlement day**

2. The payment of monies owed by one party to another.
3. The dispersal of property made by deed or will where a trust is set up. The beneficiaries are the persons who gain from the settlement and the person setting up the trust and providing the property for settlement is the ***settlor***.

**settlement day**
The day on which purchased securities are due for delivery to the buyer and payment is due to be made to the seller.

**settlement options [USA]**
The various options available to the beneficiaries of a life insurance policy in the event of the death of the insured. For example a lump sum or an income.

**settlor**
A person who sets up a trust or makes a ***settlement*** by means of money or property.

**share**
A unit of ownership in a corporation or company, ***mutual fund*** or ***limited partnership***.

**share account [UK]**
A ***building society*** account where there is no cheque book facility. Interest is usually variable and sometimes there is a notice period for withdrawals. Share account holders are members of the society and are entitled to vote and attend annual general meetings.

**share capital**
The proportion of a company's ***capital*** which derives from the issue of ***shares***, the most common being ***common stock*** and ***preferred stock (USA)*** and ***ordinary shares*** and ***preference shares (UK)***. See ***capital structure***.

### share certificate
A certificate denoting ownership of shares in a particular company. The current trend is away from paper certificates towards nominee accounts.

### share index
An index representing the combination of a number of specified company share values. For example the ***Dow Jones Industrial Average*** is the main USA share index which monitors the movement of 30 particular industrial companies traded on the ***New York Stock Exchange***. The ***FT-SE 100 Index*** is a measure of the combined share prices of the 100 largest companies (by market capitalisation) in the UK. Such indices are constantly updated with a view to tracking changes.

### share option [UK]
An incentive given to company directors and employees to promote loyalty and commitment. The scheme works by way of the employee being offered shares in the company at a fixed price (at or below the market price) for a specified time, for example five years. The option to purchase may be exercised at any time (or stated times) during this period. If the company is trading profitably and expanding the share price may well increase substantially over the option period thus providing a valuable capital gain for the employee should he/she decide to sell. Tax liabilities may be reduced on gains where schemes are approved by HM Revenue & Customs. Known as a ***stock option*** in the USA.

### share price total return
The gain (or loss) on a share price including the reinvestment of dividends into additional shares over a given period of time. The term is often used by ***investment trusts***.

## shared appreciation mortgage (SAM) [USA]
A mortgage in which a borrower pays a below normal rate of interest to the lender on the understanding that the latter shares a proportion of the appreciation of the property.

## shareholder
The owner of shares in a company.

## shell company
A company which exists in name only and which has ceased to trade. Such a company can be sold to new owners at a lower cost than setting up a new business.

## short
See *short position*.

## short bond [USA]
A bond with a near maturity date, generally under two years.

## shorts [UK]
1) Redeemable *gilts* or *bonds* with a redemption date within five years.
2) *Securities, commodities* or *financial instruments* held in a short position.

## short position
The selling of a *security, commodity* or *financial instrument* (for example, currencies etc.) which may not be owned by the seller in the belief that the price will fall. The seller would then hope to buy it back at a lower price and thus make a profit. See *long position*.

## short term debt [USA]
Debts (or *current liabilities*) falling due within one year.

**sickness benefit [UK]**
See *incapacity benefit*.

**sickness insurance**
See *permanent health insurance*. See *personal accident* and *sickness insurance*.

**simple interest**
Interest, normally paid annually, which is earned on deposited capital only, that is, unlike *compound interest*, the annual interest is not added to the capital for the purpose of calculating further interest.

**simple reversionary bonus [UK]**
See *reversionary bonus*.

**simplified employee pension plan (SEP) [USA]**
A pension plan, set up by an employee, in which both employer and employee contribute to an Individual Retirement Account (IRA).

**single premium life insurance**
A single payment for an insurance policy rather than regular premiums.

**single premium bond**
See *investment bond*.

**slump**
A severe recession over a lengthened period.

**social security disability income insurance [USA]**
Insurance which provides income to disabled persons incapacitated for one year or more. Benefits are payable up to the person's death.

### social security tax [USA]
A federal tax imposed on income and paid equally by employer and employee up to a maximum income level. Also payable by the self-employed.

### soft dollars [USA]
Payment to a broker by a customer by way of commission charges for services provided rather than a fee (known as hard dollars).

### special bonus [UK]
An additional bonus (that is, over and above the normal reversionary bonus) applied to a with profits life assurance policy when the life company's profits are exceptional.

### specialist [USA]
A member of a stock exchange who provides an orderly market in one or more securities. A specialist executes limit orders and buys and sells securities when abnormal fluctuations occur to maintain stability.

### specialised mutual fund [USA]
See *sector fund*.

### specific legacy
See *legacy*.

### speculation
The buying and/or selling of securities, commodities, currencies etc with a view to making relatively quick profits as opposed to long term investment. This type of trading is particularly prevalent in markets such as commodity futures and options.

## split [USA]

The issuing of additional shares by a corporation to its shareholders in proportion to their existing holdings but resulting in a correspondingly lower market price and as such no change in the value of the shareholders' equity. In a two for one split, original ownership of 1,000 shares at $10 per share changes to 2,000 shares at $5 per share.

## split capital investment trust (split-level trust) [UK]

An investment trust with a limited life, in which the equity capital is divided into various classes of income shares and capital shares. Holders of income shares receive the majority of the trust's income throughout its life and a specified capital amount on liquidation. Holders of capital shares receive virtually no income during the trust's life but on liquidation receive all the assets after repayment of capital to holders of income shares. These trusts are becoming more complicated in that they can now provide shares which offer income and capital at different levels of return and risk.

## spot

Another word for immediate.

## spot market

A market in the underlying instrument (for example, shares, commodities etc) on which a futures or options contract is based. This market is for immediate delivery as opposed to future delivery. Also known as cash market or physical market.

## spot price

The price of the underlying instrument (for example, shares, commodities etc) in a spot market.

## spousal IRA [USA]

An individual retirement account set up on behalf of a non-working spouse.

## spread
The difference between the buying price and selling price of a security.

## stag
A person who applies for shares in a new issue with the intention of selling them soon after trading begins. This is in the hope that the price will have immediately increased to provide a quick profit.

## stagflation
Economic stagnation (or recession) combined with inflation.

## stakeholder pension [UK]
A form of personal pension introduced in 2001 to encourage people, particularly in lower earning groups, to contribute more towards their pensions. They have low maximum charges, low minimum contribution levels, and no entry or exit charges.

## stamp duty land tax [UK]
A tax imposed when property (real estate) changes hands, payable by the purchaser. It is payable as a percentage of the purchase price, starting at 1% for properties over £125,000, up to 4% above £500,000.

## stamp duty reserve tax [UK]
A tax payable on the transfer of securities, payable by the purchaser. The rate is 0.5% of market value for shares and 1.5% for bearer instruments.

## Standard and Poor's Composite Index (S&P 500)
An index of the share prices of 500 US companies reflecting the general trend of the US stock market. The index covers

the shares of industrial, transport, utilities and financial corporations.

### standing order [UK]
An order by a customer to his/her banker to pay a specified amount usually on or around a particular day of the month regularly to another account. This could be typically for regular payment of mortgage interest or for premiums for life assurance. If the payee requires payments to be increased (or decreased) it must write to the customer requesting a change in the amount of the standing order. The customer then instructs his/her bank accordingly. Its use has been largely replaced by the *direct debit* where the customer agrees to the payee debiting (claiming funds from) his/her account.

### statement
See *statement of account* and *bank statement*.

### statement of account
A document, issued by a supplier to its customer, listing transactions over a given period, normally monthly. It will include details of invoices, payments received and any credits approved with a resultant balance payable by the customer.

### State Pension [UK]
The *pension* which is payable to persons at retirement age currently 60 for women (increasing to 65 by 2020) and 65 for men, funded by National Insurance contributions. There are two main pensions; the *basic pension* and an additional pension, currently the State Second Pension (S2P). Earlier additional pension schemes are Graduated Pension and the State Earnings Related Pension Scheme (SERPS). Pensioners can if they wish continue in employment even when they are receiving the NI Pension. See *pension forecast*.

## statutory sick pay (SSP) [UK]
Sick pay made is paid by employers to employees who are unable to work for more than three consecutive days due to illness or injury. SSP is payable for the first 28 weeks of absence after which incapacity benefit becomes payable. SSP payments to employees are taxable and subject to national insurance in the same way as normal earnings.

## stepped interest debenture stocks [UK]
A debenture stock where the rate of interest payable to lenders is increased in stages over the initial life until a certain rate is reached. Thereafter, the rate remains fixed until the redemption date. This type of debenture is advantageous to an investment trust in that interest payments will be lower than the norm in the initial years (whilst the trust consolidates its growth) and above the norm in the later years (when it will be expected that the trust's assets can afford the extra interest).

## stepped preference shares
Preference shares with dividends which increase annually by a specified amount and with a predetermined capital return.

## sterling
The currency of the UK (the UK pound). Although a long-time member of the EU, Britain did not join the euro-zone when the euro was adopted as a common currency by the majority of EU states.

## stock [USA]
Shares in a corporation conferring ownership on the holder. The two main types of stock are common stock and preferred stock. Owners of common stock are entitled to vote at shareholder meetings and to receive a dividend if payable. Owners of preferred stock receive an annual dividend

before common stockholders and priority in the event of the liquidation of a company. However they do not, as a rule, have voting rights.

**[UK]** Fixed interest securities such as gilts. There is normally a redemption date when the par value is repaid to whoever is the holder at the time. They are traded on stock exchanges where their prices fluctuate according to demand, influencing factors including interest rates and time to redemption.

**stock dividend [USA]**
The payment of a dividend to shareholders in the form of stock instead of cash. If a company declares a 5% stock dividend, a shareholder with 1,000 shares will receive an additional 50 shares. Known as a scrip dividend in the UK.

**stock exchange**
A market where securities are bought and sold. In the USA, the New York Stock Exchange is the largest exchange and in the UK, the London Stock Exchange is the equivalent largest exchange.

**Stock Exchange Automated Quotation system (SEAQ)**
The computerised system at the London Stock Exchange which continuously updates prices and trade reports for UK securities (shares, gilts etc). SEAQ lists the market makers' bid and offer prices.

**Stock Exchange Daily Official List**
See *Daily Official List*.

**Stock Exchange Pool Nominee (SEPON)**
The nominee company where all stocks and shares are held during the course of settlement on the London Stock Exchange.

### stock in trade
Raw materials and finished products carried in stock by a company. These would be included in the company's assets on the balance sheet.

### stock option [USA]
An incentive given to executives and employees to promote loyalty and commitment. The scheme works by way of the employee being offered shares in the company at a fixed price (at or below the market price) for a specified time, for example five years. The option to purchase may be exercised at any time (or stated times) during this period. If the company is trading profitably and expanding, the share price may well increase substantially over the option period thus providing a valuable capital gain for the employee. A qualified stock option is not subject to tax at the grant date or when exercised. See *option*.

### stock symbol
An abbreviation of letters allocated to a company by the exchange on which its stock is traded.

### stock transfer form
The form which the seller of a security (the transferor) signs when transferring his/her holding to a new owner (the transferee), who also signs.

### stock warrant [USA]
A transferable security often issued with preferred stock or a bond which grants the owner the right to purchase a related quantity of common stock at a specific price at a future date. Some warrants do not have a maturity date. No dividends are payable, nor are there voting rights.

### stockbroker
A broker dealing in stocks and shares on behalf of a client. In the UK, after the reorganisation of the stock market in October 1986, (known as big bang) many stockbrokers have become market makers, that is, in addition to buying and selling shares on behalf of private and institutional investors (for which a commission is charged) they can now hold shares on their own account which allows them to buy and sell to make a profit.

### stop-loss order
An order placed by an investor indicating the amount he/she is prepared to lose on a particular investment. It could be specified as 10% below the purchase price. For example if an investor purchases shares at 100p each with a stop loss order as indicated then if the share price falls to 90p it will signal the order to sell to limit his/her loss. Also a stop loss order can be placed to track the share price. In this case the order to sell would be triggered when the share price falls 10% below its highest value. For example if the shares were to increase to 125p and subsequently fall by 10% to 112.5p the order would be invoked to sell.

### straddle
The simultaneous buying of a call and a put option in the same underlying instrument (for example, shares, commodities etc) with the same expiry month and the same exercise price.

### street name [USA]
The securities of an individual held in the name of a broker or other nominee rather than the name of the individual.

### strike price
See *exercise price*.

## STRIPS

**STRIPS**
Separate Trading of Registered Interest and Principal of Securities. A system that enables investors to hold and to trade the interest and principal of specified Treasury stocks and bonds as if they were separate securities. They are not issued separately, but are purchased through financial institutions that artificially manufacture the two separate markets.

**subscription price**
The price an investor pays for shares in a new issue.

**subscription terms**
The terms under which an investor can subscribe for shares in a new issue.

**suitability [UK]**
The requirement of the *FSA* that a financial adviser must explain to a client, in a suitability report, why a recommended product is appropriate to the client's needs and circumstances.

**sum assured [UK]**
In a life assurance policy (for example, whole life assurance or endowment assurance), the sum assured is the minimum amount payable to the assured or his/her dependants on the death of the life assured.

**superannuation [UK]**
An occupational pension scheme.

**support level**
The price level at which a security stops falling.

**surrender**
The encashment of a life policy, for example an endowment assurance policy, by the assured, prior to its maturity.

**surrender value [USA]**
The amount of cash available upon the termination of a cash value insurance policy.
[UK] The cash value of, for example, an endowment assurance policy at any time throughout the term prior to its maturity. During the early years of the term the surrendering of such policies results in very little return compared with premiums paid. See *traded endowment policy* and *paid up policy*.

**swap**
The selling of one security and the buying of another in order to realise a higher yield. Other transactions can also be swapped: see currency swap and interest rate swap.

**switching**
The transferring of assets from one mutual fund or unit trust to another within a range of funds with differing objectives such as bonds, capital growth, chemicals, overseas capital growth, all managed by the same mutual fund company or unit trust institution. In the USA, switching can normally be conducted with no charge in a no load range of funds. In a range of load funds a charge is usually incurred. In the UK it is usually the case that one switch per year can be made without cost. Thereafter a charge will be made to the investor.

*take home pay*

# T

**take home pay**
The amount of money available after all deductions from salary. In the US, the most significant deductions are federal, state and local taxes, pension plan and health insurance. In the UK, the main deductions are income tax, national insurance and pension contributions.

**tangible assets**
Physical assets owned by a company or individual which can be seen or touched such as stock, machinery etc. See *intangible assets*.

**taxable earnings**
See *taxable income*.

**taxable income**
That part of a person's income which is liable to tax. In the US, this is *adjusted gross income* less allowable *deductions*. In the UK, taxable income = *gross income* - tax free pay. Tax free pay = *allowances* less deductions.

**taxable pay**
See *taxable income*.

**tax allowances [UK]**
These are allowances offset against a person's gross earnings or *gross income*. From these allowances, deductions (for example, *benefits in kind*) are subtracted in order to determine tax free pay. There are basically two types of allowances that is, those of a personal nature which are sums

fixed by the government for all individuals who qualify (for example, personal allowance) and those of a non personal nature sometimes known as charges to income or reliefs (for example, premiums paid to a personal pension plan).

## taxation
A levy on persons and companies by a government so as to finance expenditure. In the US, the main taxes are income tax, sales tax and property tax. In the UK, taxation on companies (that is, limited or public limited companies) is known as *corporation tax* and is payable on profits. Taxation on individuals may be classified as being direct or indirect, for example in the UK:

**Direct taxation:** *Income tax*, *capital gains tax*, *inheritance tax*, *council tax* and *national insurance*.
**Indirect taxation:** *Value added tax (VAT)* and *stamp duty land tax*.

## taxation schedules [UK]
Formerly, different forms of income (e.g. earned income, investment income, rental income) were classified for taxation purposes under six schedules (A to F) but these are no longer used. The taxation of different forms of income is now covered by the Income Tax (Earnings and Pensions) Act 2003 and the Income Tax (Trading and Other Income) Act 2005.

## taxation schedules [USA]
Tax forms for listing various income schedules.
*Schedule A:* Itemized deductions.
*Schedule B:* Interest and dividend income.
*Schedule C:* Profit or loss from business.
*Schedule D:* Capital gains and losses.
*Schedule E:* Supplemental income and loss.
*Schedule SE:* Social Security Self Employment tax.

### tax avoidance
The minimising of tax liability using legal methods in a manner open to the Taxation Authorities. See *tax evasion*.

### tax brackets
The ranges of *taxable income* within which particular rates of income tax are payable.

### tax codes [UK]
Under the *PAYE* system of taxing income, tax codes are allocated annually to employees. These codes enable the employer to deduct tax at the correct rate from salaries or wages on a monthly (or weekly) basis for remittance to *HM Revenue & Customs*. Most codes depict a number followed by a letter. The number refers to the amount of salary payable free of tax (for example if a person's code is 45OH, the tax free allowance will be between £4,500 and £4,509 that is, the first three numbers of the net allowances form the number of the code). The letter denotes that various personal and other allowances are included.

### tax credit [USA]
A specific dollar reduction in tax liability. For example, a taxpayer with a liability of $11,000 and a tax credit of $600 would actually be required to pay $10,400. In the case of a tax deduction the amount in question is deducted from *adjusted gross income* to reduce taxable pay on which tax is then computed.
[UK] Similarly in the UK, that amount which is deductible from a tax liability. For example, when a company pays a *dividend* to its shareholders, tax is first deducted. This deduction is then treated as a tax credit against a person's overall annual tax liability.

## tax deductible [USA]
An expense which is allowed as a deduction from *adjusted gross income* to reduce *taxable income*. For example, mortgage interest and state and local taxes.

## tax deferred [USA]
An investment such as an *individual retirement account* or *Keogh Plan* which is allowed to grow tax free until such time as benefits are taken. Tax is then payable.

## tax evasion
The minimising of tax liability by failing to declare taxable income or taxable capital gains or by submitting false information to the Taxation Authorities. This is a serious criminal offence with severe consequential penalties. See tax avoidance.

## tax exempt
Free of tax. For example, in the USA most *municipal bonds* are not subject to federal taxes on the interest.

## Tax Exempt Special Savings Account (TESSA) [UK]
Formerly a five year tax-free savings scheme, TESSAs were discontinued in 1999 and replaced by cash ISAs.

## tax exile
A wealthy person who lives outside his/her own country in order to minimise taxes. Countries which operate a low rate of tax are known as *tax havens*.

## tax free pay [UK]
A person's *allowances* less *deductions*.

## tax haven
A country where companies or individuals may legally take advantage of lower taxation levels.

**tax liability**
A legal obligation to Taxation Authorities for taxes owed.

**tax rate bands**
See *tax brackets*.

**tax relief**
The deduction of certain types of expenditure from gross salary or company profits to limit tax payable. For example pension contributions up to a certain level may be deducted from gross income to reduce taxable pay. In the UK, tax relief at the basic rate of tax is obtained by deduction from contributions paid to the pension provider, who reclaims it from *HM Revenue & Customs*.

**tax return**
A form on which certain taxpayers annually list their salary (including pensions), or income from self employment together with benefits in kind, other income and capital gains. This information is used by the Taxation Authorities to assess tax liability.

**tax voucher**
A paper advice slip issued by companies when paying *dividends* to its shareholders. The voucher indicates a number of items including the date, the dividend rate in pence per share, whether the dividend is interim or final, the number of shares held by the shareholder, the net dividend payable and the *tax credit*.

**tax year [UK]**
The twelve month period commencing 6th April and ending 5th April the following year.

## technical analysis
The study of the prices of securities, commodities and currencies etc using past history and charts (see chartist) in order to assess both value-for-money and future trends.

## telegraphic transfer
A method of transferring money abroad from one bank to another by telegraphy. In the UK, this usually refers to a transfer by the Clearing House Automated Payments System (CHAPS).

## temporary annuity
See *annuity*.

## tenancy agreement
An agreement whereby land/property is leased.

## tenancy at will
The occupancy of property by a tenant for an unspecified period. The tenancy can be terminated by either the landlord or tenant at any time.

## tenancy in common
A situation where two or more persons own land/property. In the event of the death of one of the owners, his/her interest passes to his/her estate and not the other tenants.

## tenant
A person who occupies land/property on a *lease* basis.

## tender
1. A written quotation submitted by a person or company in competition with others in order to attempt to win a contract. Usually (but not always), the company with the lowest tender is awarded the contract.

**tender offer**

2. In share dealing an offer by tender relates to potential buyers specifying the price at which they are prepared to purchase, the highest bidder being awarded the shares. In some cases buyers are asked to bid above a minimum price.

**tender offer**
See *tender 2*.

**term**
A specified period of time (that is, the term). See *term life insurance/term assurance*.

**term life insurance [USA] term assurance [UK]**
A *life insurance* policy in which cover is provided for a specified period of time (the term). The death benefit (UK *sum assured*) is paid if the death of the *insured* (UK *life assured*) occurs during the term. If the insured survives the term, the contract ceases and no benefit is payable.

**terminal bonus [UK]**
An additional bonus paid to reflect the overall performance of a *with profits* life assurance policy at *maturity* or prior death of the *life assured*. See *reversionary bonus*.

**testament**
A *will*.

**testate**
The situation which exists when a person dies having made a valid will. See *intestate*.

**testator**
A person who makes a *will*.

**testatrix**
The feminine form of *testator*.

**thin market**
A market in which unusually few transactions occur. This may apply to the shares of a specific company or the market as a whole.

**third market**
The trading of exchange listed securities in the *over the counter* market.

**third party**
The person who claims against an insured person when loss or damage to property or injury has occurred as a result of the insured person's negligence. See *third party insurance*.

**third party fire and theft**
See *motor insurance*.

**third party insurance**
The insurance of a person's legal liability (that is, a contract between an *insurer* and the *insured* person) to cover against causing injury to another person or persons (the *third party*) or loss or damage to their property. An example in the UK is third party *motor insurance*. In the event of the insured causing damage to a third party's vehicle, his/her insurers would be liable to reimburse the third party. However the insured would not be able to claim for damages to his/her vehicle. *Comprehensive insurance* would be required for this.

**thrift institution [USA]**
A depository organisation for savings including *savings and loan associations* and *mutual savings banks*. Deposits are in the main used for home mortgage loans.

**tick**
1. An upward or downward movement in the price of a security.
2. The minimum price fluctuation of a *futures* or *options contract*.

**ticker tape [USA]**
The machine which displays stock symbols, prices and volumes and transmits worldwide. Effectively replaced by computer-based systems.

**tied agent**
See *company representative*.

**time deposit [USA]**
A *savings account* or *certificate of deposit* whose funds are subject to notice (such as 30 days) prior to withdrawal. In the event of early withdrawal a penalty will normally be incurred.

**time to expiry**
The time remaining before a *warrant* is due to expire. After the expiry date a warrant has no value.

**time value**
1. The amount by which an option's *premium(4)* exceeds its *intrinsic value(1)*. Time value reflects the remaining life of an *option*.
2. The value attached to a *warrant* by virtue of its *time to expiry*. For example, a warrant which can be exercised during the month of September for any of the forthcoming five years would have a greater time value than if its expiry date was one year hence.

**title**
The right to legal ownership of *property*.

## top slicing [UK]

A method of calculating the *income tax* liability on the proceeds of *life assurance* policies. Although income tax is not normally payable on benefits from *qualifying policies*, liabilities may exist if the policy is cashed in early, that is, within ten years (or within 75% of the policy term if this happens to be shorter) or if it becomes a *paid up policy*. The proceeds of *non qualifying life policies* are liable to income tax. Assessment of income tax is on the *chargeable gain* (which is the amount of the policy proceeds less total *premiums (1)* paid) if a *chargeable event* occurs.

## total return

The return on an investment allowing not only for capital appreciation but also for any income received.

## toxic assets

Assets that expose their holders to large potential losses, such as securities backed by poor quality residential mortgages.

## tracker fund

A fund which invests to perform in line with a stock exchange index such as the *Standard and Poor's 500 Composite Index* or the *FT-SE 100*. The performance of such a fund will accordingly 'track' the index in question. Also known as an index fund.

## traded endowment policy

An endowment policy that has been sold prior to its maturity date, normally to a firm that specialises in such purchases. The policyholder usually obtains a higher figure than would be gained by surrendering the policy to the life assurance company.

### traded options
*Options* on shares, currencies, commodities which are themselves traded on an exchange.

### trade reference
A reference given by one company to another regarding the creditworthiness of another company whom it supplies with goods. It is usual for two or more trade references together with a bank reference to be requested by companies prior to supplying goods or services on credit.

### Tradepoint Investment Exchange
A former London based securities exchange that merged with the SWX Swiss Exchange to form virt-x, now renamed SWX Europe.

### trading unit [USA]
The minimum number of shares, bonds or commodities which are traded in a transaction on an exchange. This number is usually 100 for shares.

### traditional options
*Options* on shares which, unlike *traded options*, are not transferable and must be exercised on specific dates. In order to make a profit, the owner of the options has to purchase them (assuming the option price is attractive on the relevant date) and then sell them on the market.

### tranche [USA]
One of a combined group of related securities which offer various risk, reward and maturity alternatives.
[UK] A portion or slice. The term could be typically used to describe part of a *privatisation* which is being offered in stages.

**transfer**
The change of ownership of property.

**transfer agent [USA]**
An agent such as a bank which acts for a corporation in relation to the maintaining of records of stock and bond owners and other associated matters such as lost certificates.

**transfer payments [USA]**
A transfer of money from the government to individuals, typically Social Security, disability payments and unemployment benefits.

**transfer tax [USA]**
A federal tax imposed on the purchase of securities. Similar to *stamp duty reserve tax* in the UK.

**transfer value [UK]**
The value of a *pension* fund which would be available for transfer into an alternative type of plan either with the same or an alternative pension provider.

**travel insurance**
Insurance which gives cover to persons travelling usually to foreign countries on holidays or business travel. Some of the benefits include reimbursement for medical expenses, loss of luggage and money, cancellation or curtailment, departure delay and loss of passport etc. Lump sums are payable for personal accident covering death, loss of limbs or eyes or permanent disablement. Certain legal expenses for claims against a third party causing injury to the *insured* are also payable plus personal liability cover if the insured causes injury to a third party or their property. The maximum amounts of cover for all the above cases are stipulated by the insurers.

*traveler's checks*

**traveler's checks [USA] traveller's cheques [UK]**
Checks issued by *credit card* and *charge card* companies and banks etc which enable the holder to obtain cash or pay for goods and services when visiting a foreign country. The checks are signed by the traveler on their receipt and again when payment is being made. They are covered against loss provided the issuing company is notified within a specified period.

**Treasury Bill [UK]**
A government security usually with a life of 3 months but also up to one year maturity. Such bills are issued by the government at a discount and redeemable at *par* with no interest payable. They provide a principle way of financing borrowing. Other methods of government borrowing include the issuing of *gilt edged stocks* (gilts) usually fixed interest, with a variety of *redemption dates*.

**Treasury securities (treasuries) [USA]**
Debt obligations issued by the US government and secured by *full faith and credit*. Income from treasuries is subject to federal tax but not state and local taxes. They fall into four categories: Treasury bills (or T-bills, with terms of 3, 6 and 12 months), Treasury notes (with terms from one to ten years), and Treasury bonds (with terms of ten years or more) and Treasury Inflation-protected Securities (or TIPS, which are 5, 10 or 20-year bonds with the value of the principal linked to the *Consumer Price Index)*.

**trust**
An arrangement, set up by the settlor, who is the original owner of certain assets, which empowers one or more persons (the *trustees*) to safeguard those assets (within a trust fund) on behalf of another person or persons (the *beneficiaries*) under the terms of a legal document (the *trust deed*).

***turnover***

**trust deed**
The legal document which sets out the terms of a ***trust***. Included will be the names of the ***trustees*** and ***beneficiaries*** and details of the trust property/monies.

**trustee**
A person appointed to manage and safeguard the assets of a ***trust***.

**turnover [USA]**
The volume of trading in shares expressed as a percentage of total shares listed on an exchange for a specific period, for example, a day.
**[UK]** A company's total sales figure for a given trading period, normally one year.

**uberrimae fidei**
See *utmost good faith*.

**umbrella personal liability insurance [USA]**
*Liability insurance* giving excess cover over and above that cover provided by other policies. For example if general policies give total liability insurance cover of $400,000, an umbrella policy could typically provide cover of $1 million. If a claim of $700,000 were made the umbrella policy would pay out only after the $400,000 has been first exhausted.

**uncovered**
See *naked*.

**undated stocks**
Fixed interest stocks which have no *redemption date*.

**underlying instrument**
The instrument, such as shares and commodities on which a *futures* or *options contract* is based.

**underwriter**
1. A financial institution which, in return for a fee or commission (underwriting commission) agrees to purchase unsold shares in a *new issue*.
2. A person or company who assesses risk with regard to an item to be insured and if acceptable accordingly calculates the premium payable.

## underwriting commission
See *underwriter 1*.

## unearned income
Income which has not been earned by working, such as dividends from shares and interest from deposits or bonds.

## unemployment benefit [USA]
Unemployment Compensation is a benefit payable to unemployed workers, typically for up to 26 weeks. It is administered by the governments of individual states, and is usually funded by a tax on employers.
[UK] Contribution-based Jobseekers' Allowance is available for up to six months to formerly employed persons who are unemployed and are actively seeking work.

## unfranked income
Investment income received on which tax has not been paid.

## unfunded pension plan [USA]
A pension plan which is funded by an employer from current income for the benefit of retirees. Most countries do not permit private occupational pensions schemes to be unfunded, but in the UK, for instance, schemes for many state employees such as teachers and health workers are unfunded.

## unified tax credit [USA]
A federal tax credit which may be deducted from estate tax and gift tax liability.

## uninsured motorist coverage [USA]
Automobile insurance which gives cover to the insured and passengers in the event of vehicle damage and personal injury caused by an uninsured motorist.

**unissued stock [USA]**
A corporation's *authorized stock* which is as yet unissued.

**unit linked**
See *unit linked policy*.

**unit linked endowment assurance**
See *endowment assurance*.

**unit linked life assurance**
See *unit linked policy*.

**unit linked policy [UK]**
1. A *life assurance* policy in which a portion of the *premium(1)* is used to purchase life cover (the *sum assured*) with the balance invested in an authorised *unit trust*/trusts or the insurance company's own internal funds. The return on the policy is thus linked to the performance of the units in the unit trust. Unit linked policies include single premium bonds or *investment bonds*, unit linked endowment assurance and unit linked whole life assurance. See endowment assurance. See whole life assurance.
2. A *pension* plan in which members' contributions are used to purchase units in an *authorised unit trust*.

**unit linked whole of life assurance**
See *whole life assurance*.

**unit of trading [USA]**
The minimum number of shares, bonds or commodities which are traded in a transaction on an exchange. This number is usually 100 for shares.

## unit trust [UK]

A collective investment scheme which enables small private investors to invest directly in a diversified portfolio of shares. It is known as an *open end* fund since there is no fixed amount of *capital* in the trust. Management is by professional fund managers who invest in securities to achieve the trust's objectives such as capital growth, income or a combination of both. The *trustees*, typically a bank, ensure the managers operate the trust in accordance with the *trust deed*. Each investor is allocated units in the trust which represent the amount of his/her investment at the time of purchase. The price at which units are sold to investors is known as the offer price or buying price. When such units are ultimately sold by the investor the price obtained is known as the bid price or selling price. The difference between the offer and bid prices is known as the *bid/offer* spread. Bid and offer prices of authorised and other unit trusts are published daily in leading newspapers such as the Financial Times, which enable the investor to regularly check on the value of his/her units.

## unitisation

The conversion of an *investment trust* into *unit trust*.

## unitised with profits [UK]

A form of hybrid between with profits and unit-linked policies. As with unit-linked, premiums are used to purchase units in a fund and the amount of a claim payment depends on the number and value of units. The value of units, however, increases with the addition of bonuses which, like reversionary bonuses on with profits, cannot be removed.

## universal life insurance [USA]

A combination of *term life insurance* and a savings element which is invested to provide a cash value build up. The policy is flexible in that the death benefit, savings element and premiums can be reviewed and altered from time to time as a policyholder's circumstances change.

### unlisted securities [USA]
Securities which are not traded on a main exchange such as the *New York Stock Exchange*. Instead they are traded in the *over the counter* market.
[UK] Shares (usually in small companies) which are not listed on a *Recognised Investment Exchange*.

### unlisted securities market
A market set up by the *London Stock Exchange* in 1980 for the trading of shares of small to medium sized companies which did not qualify for a full *listing*. The USM was discontinued at the end of 1996 and replaced by the alternative investment market (AIM).

### unpaid dividend
A dividend which has been declared by a corporation but as yet unpaid.

### unsecured loan
A loan where the lender has no entitlement to any of the borrower's assets in the event of the borrower failing to make the loan repayments, and therefore relies solely on the borrower's agreement to repay set out in the loan contract. Such a loan normally carries a higher interest rate than a *secured loan*.

### unsecured loan stock
*Loan stock* issued by a company but without security, that is, the holder of the loan stock does not have entitlement to any of the company's assets in the event of non repayment of the loan.

**upper earnings limit [UK]**
The earnings level of an employee above which a reduced rate of Class 1 *National Insurance contributions* is payable.

**U S Federal Reserve**
See *Federal Reserve*.

**utilities**
Companies which provide essential services such as electricity, gas and water.

**utmost good faith**
All contracts of insurance are subject to utmost good faith in that persons are obliged to disclose any detail which may be of importance to the insurers whether or not it is requested.

*valuation*

**valuation**
The *value* or worth of a *portfolio* of investments recorded on a statement.

**value**
The worth or desirability of something expressed as an amount of money.

**value added tax (VAT) [UK]**
An indirect tax levied on goods and services in the UK. A company or trader registered for VAT pays suppliers VAT additionally to the cost of goods or services purchased which is known as *input tax*. Also VAT is added to the sales cost of their product when invoicing customers which is known as *output tax*. The difference between output tax and input tax is payable to HM Revenue & Customs.

**valued policy**
An insurance policy in which the value of the insured item is defined and agreed at the commencement of the policy. In the event of a total loss the agreed amount is paid by the insurer without the need for further proof of value.

**variable annuity**
See *annuity*.

**variable interest rate**
Interest rates offered by banks and financial institutions on loans or deposits which are liable to change according to

circumstances. For example a movement in the interest rate set by the government or central bank would usually be an influence.

**variable life insurance [USA]**
A form of *cash value life insurance* in which the cash value of the policy may be invested in shares and bonds etc. according to the insured's choice.

**variable rate certificate**
A *certificate of deposit* whose interest rate varies and is dependent on an influence such as *prime rate*.

**variable rate mortgage (VRM)**
A *mortgage* where the interest rate is not fixed and which is dependent on influences such as interest rates on *Treasury securities* in the US or *base rate* in the UK.

**variance**
The difference between budgeted and actual costs.

**variation margin**
Profits and losses on open *futures contracts*, which are revalued daily at the *settlement price*, which are subsequently paid to or received from the *clearing house*.

**vendor**
A person or company selling goods and property.

**venture capital**
Capital invested into small and young companies in return for equity ownership. Such companies, often manufacturing high technology products, have potential for significant growth but at much higher risk.

### venture capital trust [UK]
A company similar to an *investment trust* in which the majority of its capital is invested in small unquoted companies (companies whose shares are not quoted on a *Recognised Investment Exchange*). There is a limit on how much may be invested in a single company and a limit on the capital value of companies in which the trust may invest funds. Since this type of trust invests in a range of companies the risk involved with *venture capital* tends to be spread.

### vesting
Conversion. For example the vesting of a pension fund is its conversion into a pension.

### Visa
An international card scheme providing a range of payment services.

### VocaLink
Established in 1969 as Bankers Automated Clearing Services (BACS), VocaLink operates as the UK clearing system for automated payments such as direct debits and direct credits.

### volatility
The significant price variations of a security, commodity or market as a whole over a short period of time. Large fluctuations reflect high volatility.

### volume
A reference to the amount of shares traded on a stock exchange for a given period.

### voluntary deductible employee contribution plan [USA]
A type of pension plan in which an employee elects to have regular payments deducted from each paycheck.

## voluntary liquidation [USA]
The liquidation of a company approved by its shareholders.
**[UK]**
1. Members' voluntary liquidation or winding up: The winding up of a company voluntarily with the directors' declaration that debts are payable.
2. Creditors' voluntary liquidation or winding up: The winding up of a company with a resolution stating the company is unable to trade due to its debts.

## voting right
The entitlement of the owner of *common stock* or *ordinary shares* to vote in person or by *proxy* at *annual meetings* or *annual general meetings*.

## voting stock [USA]
Stock, typically *common stock*, which confers on the owner the right to vote on election of directors and other corporate matters.

## voucher
A receipt for the payment of money confirming an entry in book keeping.

### waiting period [USA]
The period, prior to payments by the insurers to a policyholder of *disability income insurance* after a claim, during which no payments are made. This is typically several months. Also known as elimination period. Known as deferment period in the UK.

### waiver of premium
An arrangement in *life insurance*, which, in return for some increase in premium, ensures that policyholders have their premiums paid during periods of absence from work due to illness or accident. There is usually an elimination period (or waiting period), UK *deferment period*, typically several months, after which the insurers commence payments.

### warrant [USA]
See *stock warrants*.
[UK] A transferable security which grants the owner the right but not the obligation to purchase shares in a company at a specific price (*exercise price*) at a future date/dates, or during a future period/periods. They do not pay dividends nor do they carry voting rights. They are traded on stock exchanges. Warrants offer gearing (share price/warrant price) which results in a magnified up or down percentage movement of the warrant price following a change in share price. Most warrants are issued by *investment trusts*. See *premium*, *time value* and *intrinsic value*.

## warranty

A contract in which a seller commits to a buyer that any faulty workmanship or product failure occurring within a specified period will be rectified at no cost to the buyer. Typical products covered by warranty include appliances, automobiles and machinery.

## weak market

A stock market where volume is low and the spread is high.

## wedding insurance

Insurance to give protection against financial loss in relation to a wedding. Items typically covered include costs arising out of unavoidable cancellation, damage to hired dress wear and loss of or damage to wedding presents and wedding rings.

## white knight

A company (or person) making a welcome takeover bid usually with an improved offer for another company which has been the subject of an unwanted hostile bid from another party known as a *black knight*. See also *gray/grey knight*.

## whole life insurance [USA]

A life insurance policy, with level premiums, which provides a stated benefit on the death of the life insured and a savings element which accumulates a cash value. The cash value dividends or interest are allowed to build up tax deferred. The insured is able to redeem the cash value or borrow against it which is known as a policy loan. Any part of a loan which is unpaid at the death of the insured is deducted from the face value.

## whole life assurance [UK]

A *life assurance* policy which pays out a sum of money (the *sum assured*) on the death of the *life assured*. If a whole life

## will

policy is encashed in its early years any proceeds returnable to the policyholder will normally be below the value of the premiums paid up to cancellation.

## will

A document which sets out how a person wishes his/her estate or property to be dispersed after his/her death. The document must be signed by the *testator/testatrix* (the person making the will) in the presence of two witnesses who must also sign. An *executor* (female form *executrix*) or executors are appointed by the testator to ensure that his/her wishes are carried out.

## windfall shares [UK]

Free shares issued to members of a building society that *demutualises* and becomes a commercial bank operating as a *public limited company*.

## windfall tax [UK]

A one-off tax imposed by the government. An example is the tax imposed on the profits of privatised utility companies in 1997. A windfall tax on energy companies was proposed in 2008 during a period of high energy prices.

## winding up

See *liquidation*.

## withholding [USA]

A deduction from an employee's salary by an employer for federal, state and local tax liabilities.

## with profits [UK]

An expression referring to a *life assurance* or *pension* policy which participates in receiving part of the life company's profits which derive from investments in equities, property and fixed interest securities etc. They are paid by way of ***reversionary bonuses*** and ***terminal bonuses***. This principle is applied to ***with profits bonds***, with profits endowment assurance, with profits whole life assurance, low cost endowment assurance and with profits pension plans. See ***endowment assurance*** and ***whole life assurance***.

### with profits bond
A ***bond***, purchased with a lump sum, affiliated to ***with profits*** growth and more suitable for long term investment.

### without prejudice
Basic meaning is without loss of any rights. It is a term used in offers intended to guard against any inference of waiver of rights and in correspondence seeking to negotiate a compromise, in which case the communication so made cannot be used in evidence in court proceedings.

### working capital
A company's current assets (cash, debtors, work in progress) less its current liabilities (creditors, taxes due). This capital is used by a company to run its business.

### World Trade Organisation (WTO)
An international organization dealing with the rules of trade between nations, centred on the WTO agreements, negotiated and signed by most of the world's trading nations and ratified in their parliaments.

### writ
A written order issued by a court instructing the defendant to appear in court to answer charges made by the plaintiff.

**writer**
A person who makes an *opening sale* of an *option* contract. Upon notification of *exercise* by the option *holder* (the buyer), the writer is obliged to deliver or take delivery of the *underlying instrument* (for example, shares, commodities etc).

# XYZ

**xa [UK]**
Another way of writing ex all. This means that shares bought in a company are without entitlement to current *dividends*, *rights issues* or *scrip issues*. Such entitlement remains with the seller of the shares.

**xc**
Another way of writing ex scrip or ex capitalisation. Shares bought in a company are without entitlement to current *scrip issues*. Such entitlement remains with the seller of the shares.

**xd**
Another way of writing ex dividend. Shares bought in a company are without entitlement to current *dividends*. Such entitlement remains with the seller of the shares.

**xr**
Another way of writing ex rights. Shares bought in a company are without entitlement to current *rights issues*. Such entitlement remains with the seller of the shares.

**xw [USA]**
Another way of writing ex warrants. Shares bought in a company are without entitlement to warrants.

**yield**
The annual percentage rate of return on an investment. It is calculated by relating the annual income, and/or the amount and timing of the capital return, to the amount invested. The

yield based purely on annual income is known as the current yield or running yield; if account is taken of the future return of capital, it is known as the yield to maturity.

### zero coupon bond [USA]

A bond where no interest is paid during its life. Such a bond is purchased at a substantial discount and the accumulated interest is added to the face value at maturity. Although not paid, the annual interest is taxable as income.

[UK] A bond which pays no interest throughout its life and which pays a capital gain by being issued at a substantial discount to the maturity value. Thus there may be a liability to *capital gains tax*. Depending on circumstances this may offer an advantage to certain taxpayers since there is no income tax liability.

### zero dividend preference shares (zeros) [UK]

*Preference shares* which receive no dividends throughout their lives. Instead a fixed known amount is paid at maturity.

### zero rated [UK]

A term relating to *value added tax (VAT)*. It refers to goods (for example, food and books) which are taxable but at a zero rate. The significance of this rating is that businesses selling such goods may claim back their *input tax* (the VAT which they have paid to their suppliers). Businesses which provide goods and services which are VAT exempt (for example, stamps and postal services) are not able to reclaim input tax.